E&C E & Cº

ELKINGTON & Cº

Understanding
ANTIQUE
SILVER PLATE

This amusing electroplated egg-boiler stands on bark-textured supports and has a cast cockerel finial. The interior is fitted to hold four eggs, the heat supplied by a small spirit burner. 9in (22.9cm) tall, it was made by an unidentified maker. £200-£300.

Understanding
ANTIQUE
SILVER PLATE

STEPHEN J. HELLIWELL

ANTIQUE COLLECTORS' CLUB

© 1997 Antique Collectors' Club Ltd.
World copyright reserved

First published 1996
This reprint 2000

ISBN 1 85149 247 X

British Cataloguing-in-Publication Data
A catalogue record for this book is available from the British Library

Printed in England by the Antique Collectors' Club Ltd.
5 Church Street, Woodbridge, Suffolk IP12 1DS
on Consort Royal Satin paper
supplied by the Donside Paper Company, Aberdeen, Scotland

Contents

Introduction 9

Mercury or Fire Plating 11

Cold Gilding 14

Close Plating 15

Old Sheffield Plate or Fused Plate 19
    Early Old Sheffield Plate 25
    The Later Wares 30
    Candlesticks and Candelabra 31
    Dining Plate 50
    Cutlery 75
    Tea and Coffee Accessories 80
    Trays and Salvers 92
    Alcoholic Objects 99
    Writing Equipment 118
    Miscellaneous Pieces 122
    The Demise of Old Sheffield Plate 130
    The Care of Old Sheffield Plate 131
    Fakes and Reproductions 134

Electroplate 136
    Introduction 136
    The Process of Manufacture 138
    Early Electroplate 141
    The Later Wares 145
    Candlesticks and Candelabra 149
    Dining Plate 155
    Cutlery 171
    Tea and Coffee Accessories 174
    Trays and Salvers 187
    Alcoholic Objects 190
    Writing Equipment 197
    Miscellaneous Pieces 202

Marks on Plate 215

Illustrations of Marks 221

Glossary 226

Bibliography 229

Two wine coolers, the smaller example Old Sheffield plate, unmarked, c.1820, the larger a 20th century reproduction, confusingly stamped: 'Plate on copper, made in Sheffield'. The latter mark might lead the unwary collector to make an expensive mistake. 9in (22.9cm) and 9¾in (24.8cm) high. £400-£600 and £30-£40 for single examples.

PHOTOGRAPHIC ACKNOWLEDGEMENT

The author and the publisher would like to thank Christie's South Kensington for providing photographs for this book.

PRICE REVISION LIST

The usefulness of a book containing prices rapidly diminishes as market values change.

In order to keep the prices updated, a price revision list will be issued annually. This will record the major price changes in the values of the items covered under the various headings in the book.

To ensure that you receive the price revision list, complete the pro forma invoice inserted in this book and send it to the address below:

ANTIQUE COLLECTORS' CLUB
5 CHURCH STREET
WOODBRIDGE, SUFFOLK, IP12 1DS

Dedicated to William R. Ward

The Antique Collectors' Club

THE ANTIQUE COLLECTORS' CLUB was formed in 1966 and quickly grew to a five figure membership spread throughout the world. It publishes the only independently run monthly antiques magazine, *Antique Collecting*, which caters for those collectors who are interested in widening their knowledge of antiques, both by greater awareness of quality and by discussion of the factors which influence the price that is likely to be asked. The Antique Collectors' Club pioneered the provision of information on prices for collectors and the magazine still leads in the provision of detailed articles on a variety of subjects.

It was in response to the enormous demand for information on 'what to pay' that the price guide series was introduced in 1968 with the first edition of *The Price Guide to Antique Furniture* (completely revised 1978 and 1989), a book which broke new ground by illustrating the more common types of antique furniture, the sort that collectors could buy in shops and at auctions rather than the rare museum pieces which had previously been used (and still to a large extent are used) to make up the limited amount of illustrations in books published by commercial publishers. Many other price guides have followed, all copiously illustrated, and greatly appreciated by collectors for the valuable information they contain, quite apart from prices. The Price Guide Series heralded the publication of many standard works of reference on art and antiques. *The Dictionary of British Art* (now in six volumes), *The Pictorial Dictionary of British 19th Century Furniture Design, Oak Furniture* and *Early English Clocks* were followed by many deeply researched reference works such as *The Directory of Gold and Silversmiths*, providing new information. Many of these books are now accepted as the standard work of reference on their subject.

The Antique Collectors' Club has widened its list to include books on gardens and architecture. All the Club's publications are available through bookshops world wide and a full catalogue of all these titles is available free of charge from the addresses below.

Club membership, open to all collectors, costs little. Members receive free of charge *Antique Collecting*, the Club's magazine (published ten times a year), which contains well-illustrated articles dealing with the practical aspects of collecting not normally dealt with by magazines. Prices, features of value, investment potential, fakes and forgeries are all given prominence in the magazine.

Among other facilities available to members are private buying and selling facilities and the opportunity to meet other collectors at their local antique collectors' clubs. There are over eighty in Britain and more than a dozen overseas. Members may also buy the Club's publications at special pre-publication prices.

As its motto implies, the Club is an organisation designed to help collectors get the most out of their hobby: it is informal and friendly and gives enormous enjoyment to all concerned.

For Collectors — By Collectors — About Collecting

ANTIQUE COLLECTORS' CLUB
5 Church Street, Woodbridge Suffolk IP12 1DS, UK
Tel: 01394 385501 Fax: 01394 384434
Email: sales@antique-acc.com
Website: www.antique-com.com
—————————— or ——————————
Market Street Industrial Park, Wappingers' Falls, NY 12590, USA
Tel: 914 297 0003 Fax: 914 297 0068
E-mail: info@antiquecc.com
Website www.antiquecc.com

Introduction

Pride and ambition are essential parts of man's nature, and the history of antiques is full of attempts to 'make a silk purse from a sow's ear' for the sake of creating a good impression. Cheap materials were concealed with fashionable, expensive exteriors, and straightforward replicas in less costly substances were also produced in large quantities. Thus, 18th century and later furniture with inexpensive oak carcases was veneered with a thin layer of mahogany and other exotic woods, while Victorian parlours were bedecked with parian porcelain and spelter statuettes, closely resembling, at a glance, the marbles and bronzes they were designed to copy.

In the same way, base metals were plated with gold and silver, often in an attempt to deceive potential buyers. Certainly, as early as 1327, a complaint was made that London cutlers: "in their workhouses cover tin with silver so subtilely and with such sleight that the same cannot be discerned and severed from the tin, and by that means they sell the tin so covered as fine silver to the great damage and deceit of us and our people". Acts of Parliament were passed in the 14th century which forbade gilding of any metal other than silver, and silvering of any articles other than knights' spurs and pieces of nobles' apparel, but many unscrupulous manufacturers chose to break the law, and one can find numerous reports of infringement and subsequent punishment for the production of: "counterfeit stuff, whereby any ignorant man may be induced to take the same for silver and gold", the latter a quotation from an arbitration of 1628.

The two earliest methods of covering cheap, base metals with a thin skin of gold or silver were mercury, or fire plating, and close plating. Both techniques continued in use well into the 19th century. Old Sheffield plate, or fused plate, introduced in the mid-18th century, was soon produced in enormous quantities in both Sheffield and Birmingham. Still immensely popular, fused plate objects can, today, sell for as much as their silver counterparts. The process of electroplating on a commercial scale swept the board in the 1850s, soon replacing the more expensive Old Sheffield plate. Although still produced in large quantities, old electroplate can be very valuable, as we shall see.

Fortunately for the modern collector there is still a great deal of 18th and 19th plate on the market, although prices are now ever spiralling upwards. Only a few years ago one could still have bought cheaply, as many potential buyers tended to despise the cheaper medium, purchasing second rate antique silver rather than excellent and attractive plate. Today, however, there are many connoisseurs who collect only plate, scouring auctions, shops and markets for scarce pieces still in good condition. This new interest has lead to some inevitable increases in cost, although less unusual, cheaper items can still be found by the patient or lucky. In this book I have suggested possible retail prices for typical pieces in good, original condition, but one must always be prepared to pay more for rarities or particularly outstanding examples. Condition is of paramount importance, and worn, damaged and repaired objects should be rejected unless very cheap. Even then one should only buy if they temporarily fill a gap in an otherwise complete collection. When a better specimen turns up one will hopefully be able to sell the poorer piece, perhaps making a small profit, assuming one paid a cheap enough price originally.

Plate can be found in all outlets of antiques, from the top auction houses and shops right down to local car boot sales and flea markets. The latter are excellent

An unusual unmarked ramekin dish stand fitted with six glazed pottery dishes with covers, 10¾in (27.3cm) long. This piece bears some resemblance to the designs of Dr. Christopher Dresser and therefore probably dates to the Arts and Crafts period of the late 19th century. £300-£400.

hunting grounds for the knowledgeable collector, as some of the trade may make mistakes, selling rare items for a quick, small profit without researching them properly first. Auction rooms may hold regular sales including plate. Christies' of South Kensington, for example, sell a hundred or so plate lots in their fortnightly sales of silver, ranging from bulk lots of inexpensive E.P.N.S., ideal for everyday use, to individual pieces, selected because of their age, condition and rarity. Some dealers specialise in plate, maintaining large selections of fine fused plate and electroplate. While their prices may not seem cheap, the purchaser is guaranteed to find quality of merchandise and plenty of expertise and sound advice. The beginner should, perhaps, start off here, gleaning much invaluable knowledge before branching out on his or her own. This knowledge can only come from handling the objects themselves, preferably in the company of an expert, who can point out potential pitfalls as well as those insignificant, special features which can make one piece far more desirable than another.

As with all antiques, I feel strongly that one should use the pieces in one's collection. Obviously they must be treated with respect and care, but there is no reason why the dining table cannot be covered with dishes and candlesticks, or why one cannot enjoy tea poured from an elegant George III teapot. I am somewhat disheartened by the 'collector' who buys purely for investment, locking his treasures away in a bank vault in the hope that they will increase substantially in value. Personally, I prefer to deal with the 'lover' of old plate, who enjoys his purchases, displaying them with joy and pride, and using them with a great deal of satisfaction.

Mercury or Fire Plating

This method of plating base metals with gold or silver is probably the oldest successful method. The process is described in Cellini's treatise on metal-working, written in the 16th century, and continued in use until the introduction of electroplating in the mid-19th century, changing hardly at all over the centuries.

The Process of Manufacture.

First of all the precious metal, either gold or silver, to be used for plating an object made of base metal, was powdered, and then heated in a crucible until it became 'red hot', and then a quantity of mercury was added. The proportion of gold or silver to mercury could vary, but normally between five and eight times as much mercury was used in the amalgam. The two metals were then mixed thoroughly together until completely blended. The resultant glutinous mixture, now with a consistency approaching that of thick treacle, was washed in clean water. It was then squeezed to remove as much of the loose, surplus mercury as possible. The amalgam, now a stiff paste, was placed inside a chamois leather bag. This was also squeezed until more mercury was excluded, the liquid metal passing through the porous leather of the bag. Any mercury driven off in this way was saved for further use, as it invariably contained a small amount of reusable gold or silver in solution.

The remaining paste consisted of approximately one third precious metal to two thirds of mercury. Now with a consistency of thick clay, it was smeared on to the object to be plated, after the latter had been covered with a solution of mercury nitrate, made by dissolving a tablespoon of mercury in a quart of nitric acid. This liquid ensured that the gold or silver would bond successfully with the base metal beneath

Once the piece was covered with an even coating of amalgam, it was heated in a furnace, the heat causing the mercury to evaporate, leaving behind a thin skin of precious metal. The temperature of the furnace was regulated as closely as possible, to avoid blistering or scarring. Several attempts might have been necessary before a sufficient thickness of gold or silver was achieved. Small articles such as buttons were, apparently, covered in amalgam and then placed inside an iron frying pan. Here they were heated over an open flame "till the mercury begins to fly off", leaving behind a deposit of gold or silver.

Although it was possible to use the above process for plating with silver, mercury or fire plating was used more often for gilding, covering base metal with a thin film of gold. Obviously one could use the method to create an attractive effect when partially gilding pieces, by painting the stiff gold and mercury amalgam on to selected areas. This enabled the skilful gilder to decorate pieces with elaborate colour contrasts. It was also used extensively for lining food vessels, the thin skin of gold preventing damage to the base metal by salts or acids found in certain foodstuffs. Certainly one may find that base metal fruit stands, epergnes, salt cellars and egg cups were commonly parcel-gilt as a safety precaution, although gilding was frequently employed, particularly on larger, more spectacular, pieces, purely for its decorative effect. Needless to say, it was also used to cover objects fashioned in silver, both for decoration and as a precaution against damage, as outlined above.

A pair of brass salvers made c.1725. They can be dated quite accurately, as they are engraved with the armorial of Charles Eversfield of Horsham, Sussex, before his second marriage in 1731. Although many years of cleaning have taken their toll, close examination of the angles and the bracket feet reveals slight traces of the original silvering. These extremely rare pieces may have been mercury-plated, although some examples appear to be covered with traces of straight lines of silver, suggesting that they may have been French plated using silver leaf. To further the deception that they are made of silver, these 12in (30.5cm) salvers are struck with facsimile hallmarks – two crude lion passant punches and an unidentifiable date letter or maker's mark.(See Marks, page 215.) £2,500-£3,500.   Photo courtesy Brian Beet

Problems associated with Mercury Gilding

Although mercury or fire gilding could be used to wonderful effect, it was perhaps employed less often than one might think. This is because the process was extremely dangerous for the workmen. Not only did they actually handle the mercury, absorbing a certain amount of the toxic metal through the pores in their skin, but they also breathed in the potentially deadly mercury fumes as the metal evaporated, thus poisoning themselves over a comparatively short period of time. This pernicious threat was recognised in the early days of the plating industry, and manufacturers charged a large premium for gilt or parcel-gilt pieces. While a certain amount of the higher price was accounted for by the cost of the gold used in the process, a large percentage was also needed for higher wages, to tempt workers from less dangerous areas of manufacture into this more lucrative, high risk employment. The magazine *Silver* recently reprinted an extract of 'The Application of Art to Manufactures' written by George C. Mason and G. P. Putnam, originally printed in 1858, which described the dangers inherent in mercury plating as follows: "The old process (Mercury Gilding)....is most pernicious and destructive to human life; the mercury volatized by the heat insinuates itself into the bodies of the

Although mercury-gilding was often used to line objects, pieces entirely covered with gold are scarce. Here we see a set of six mercury-gilt copper dessert baskets measuring 11in (27.9cm) and 10in (25.4cm) in diameter. Unmarked, but made c.1790, each is engraved with a contemporary armorial with crest and motto. It is unusual to find a pair in such pristine condition, let alone a set of six, so one could expect to pay at least £3,000-£5,000 for this set.

workmen, not withstanding the greatest care; and those who are so fortunate as to escape, for a time, absolute disease, are constantly liable to salivation from its effects. Paralysis is common among them, and the average of their lives is very short – not exceeding thirty-five years, according to estimate". It is interesting to see that Mason and Putnam wrote of mercury gilding as "the old process", quite rightly condemning its dangers, but talking as if they were a thing of the past. In fact, at the time when they were writing, in the mid-19th century, the 'modern' technique of electroplating caused equally unpleasant and potentially fatal sickness amongst the workforce, as we will see in a subsequent chapter.

The Care of Mercury Plated Objects

Base metal pieces plated with silver using the method described above are now very rare and therefore costly, and it is difficult to distinguish them from objects originally sold as copper or brass when first made, and then subsequently 'enhanced' with electroplating much later on, perhaps even in this century. Mercury parcel-gilt pieces can still be found quite easily, however, as the process has proved to be extremely durable. As Frederick Bradbury wrote in 1912: "…fire-gilding…is more costly but far more lasting than the modern method of depositing the gold by electricity". In fact, one frequently finds parcel-gilt Old Sheffield Plate pieces worn almost free of silver through over-zealous cleaning, although their gilt interiors are still in very good condition, despite many years of use. Mercury gilding can be recognised by its warm, red glow, and should never by covered by electro-gilding, even if it is somewhat worn. Modern gilding lacks the depth and strength of colour, and is, to my eye at least, far less attractive. Gilt pieces are best cleaned quite simply with hot, soapy water. One should then rinse off the suds, polishing each piece with a soft, dry cloth.

Cold Gilding

This early method of plating base metal with gold did not require the use of mercury. Instead, pure gold mixed with a little copper was dissolved in aqua regia, a blend of nitric and hydrochloric acids. Once the metals were totally dissolved, the solution was dropped on to rags which were allowed to absorb the liquid. Once dried, the rags were burned, their ashes containing the gold in a powdered form. These ashes could then be rubbed on to the surface to be gilded using a damp cork, the gold sticking to the surface with a tight bond. The piece was subsequently polished with a piece of smooth bloodstone or haematite. Although described by Mason and Putnam in the work mentioned above, this method of gilding seems to have been little used, perhaps because it was inherently only suitable for covering smooth, flat surfaces. Impractical for gilding more complex, decorative shapes, it can, today, be dismissed as a curiosity, not least because it would be impossible to distinguish it from the much more common mercury gilding.

Close Plating

The early process of silvering iron or steel knights' spurs in the 14th century, mentioned above, was undoubtedly that of close plating, a technique which enabled a manufacturer to coat almost any base metal with a thin skin of silver. The method is, however, extremely time-consuming and laborious so, in practice, its use was confined to small pieces, usually with sharp cutting edges, or with pointed ends. As a result it was employed primarily for cutlery, although many other items which had to be capable of withstanding both stress and wear were also close plated. The latter category included harness fittings, spurs and stirrups, carriage door handles and candle wick-trimmers.

The Process of Manufacture

Firstly, the surface to be plated had to be perfectly smooth and clean, as any irregularities or tiny spots of dirt or grease would ruin the finished product. Once prepared, the surface was dipped into a flux of sal ammoniac, and then covered with molten tin. The latter was allowed to cool and harden, and then a piece of beaten silver foil, cut to the requisite shape, was placed evenly on to the tinned surface. The two were pressed firmly together, and then a hot soldering iron was rubbed over the surface, the heat passing through the silver foil to melt the tin, forming a solder which fused together the iron or steel and the silver. Much experience was required at this stage, as the extremely thin silver would simply melt away if the soldering iron was a few degrees too hot. When the surface had been smoothed over with the soldering iron, the edges of sheet silver were clipped away. This 'fash' was, of course, recycled. Floor sweepings were assiduously collected, the careful manufacturers melting them down for subsequent re-use. The edges of the article could now be burnished down, and then the piece was hand or machine-buffed to a fine polish.

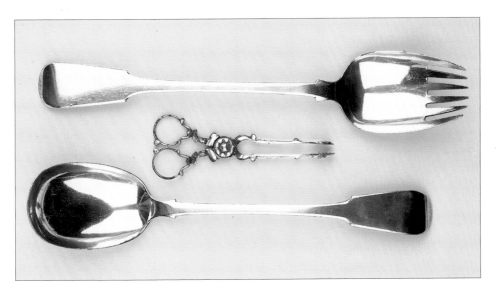

Three rare pieces of close plated iron, the pair of 12in (30.5cm) salad servers dating to c.1820, possibly by John Gilbert of Birmingham. The three items are in rather poor condition, the thin silver skin peeling away from the base metal. The servers £50-£80 the pair, the sugar nips, £20-£30.

An unmarked close-plated tea caddy made c.1790. Notice that the steel body has rusted, causing the sheet silver to lift and break away. 4½in (11.4cm) long, it is worth £150-£200.

Problems Associated with Close Plate

The thin silver foil coating used in this process is extremely fragile, melting away if exposed to direct heat. While this may not have been a problem with cutlery, one finds many wick-trimmers damaged in this way. Great care had to be taken when trimming a lighted candle, as contact with the flame inevitably resulted in blistering, and even loss, of the applied surface. Perhaps more seriously, articles made of close plate are very vulnerable to damp. Moisture penetrates the surface skin with ease, causing the metal beneath to rust and corrode. This in turn made more of the silver lift away, causing bubbling and eventual flaking. Although one may be tempted by pieces with only small traces of such damage, it can be much worse than it seems, the rust creeping along the iron beneath the silver until, one day, the entire skin crumbles away. The problem of damp has ensured the scarcity of spurs, stirrups, and other horse trappings, which would have been impossible to keep dry when they were in everyday use.

Close plated objects also had to be perfectly plain. Any engraved or chased decoration would simply lift and tear the silver skin. Indeed, many marked pieces have suffered particularly badly, their punched stamps breaking the surface to expose the metal beneath Manufacturers were able to overcome this problem to a certain extent, by affixing unadorned blades and prongs to deeply-carved, ornate handles. By the mid-19th century however, customers demanded ever more elaborate decoration, particularly on dessert services. Electroplating was able to

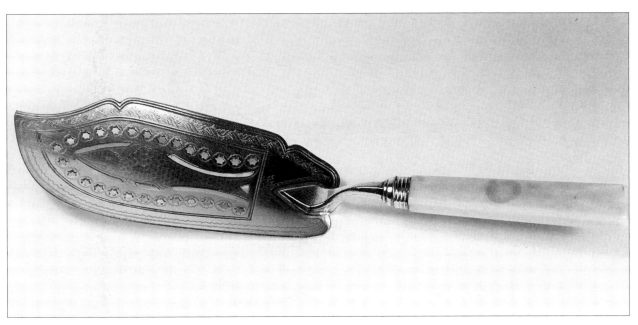

This attractive fish slice shows how well close plating can be done. It bears the mark of Birmingham close-plater John Gilbert, registered in 1812. £100-£150.

answer these demands, as pieces could be decorated with masses of frivolous trailing vines and flowers before plating. This introduction caused the start of the downfall of close plate, although some manufacturers persisted in its use until the late 19th century.

Much of the close plate one sees today has deteriorated to some extent through the ravages of damp. Such pieces are unattractive and unusable, and should be left well alone.

Close Plated Objects

Pieces enhanced with close plating were manufactured in Sheffield, Birmingham and London until the late 19th century, although, from about 1780 the process was confined largely to cutlery. One can still find a good selection of items, particularly dessert knives and forks, with carved or plain bone or mother-of-pearl handles. Most are very cheap, and one can purchase odd pieces for a few pounds. A complete set of fruit eaters would, of course, be more expensive, twelve pairs of knives and forks in a veneered box retailing for £400-500. Wick-trimmers, later examples often made of fused plate but with close plated steel blades and boxes, usually cost £50-70, while an attractive pair of grape scissors or a sturdy cheese scoop would sell for £100-150. Spurs and stirrups in good condition are very rare, for reasons described above. Nevertheless they seem to be little collected, and one could still find good examples for less than £100.

Many pieces of close plate were marked with the maker's initials or the manufacturer's name in full. These were often deliberately made to resemble hallmarks on silver, each letter stamped in a separate punch so that the ignorant could be fooled quite easily. Needless to say, this style of marking caused a great deal of ill-feeling amidst the silver trade. Other close plate makers used curious symbols as trademarks and punches, or stamped the letters 'S' or 'PS', these standing for steel or plated steel. If in doubt whether a piece is made of close plate or later electroplate one can always test it with a magnet. If it is close plate then the magnet will adhere to the iron or steel beneath the silver skin.

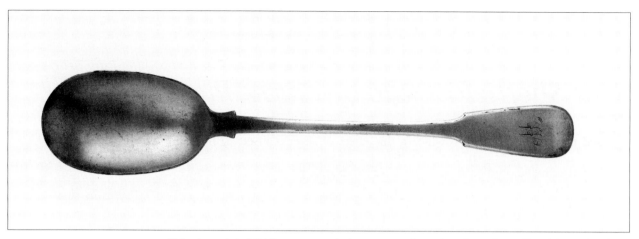

This close-plated fiddle pattern salad spoon, made c.1815, has also suffered from the effects of damp, the moisture rusting the metal beneath to make the silver skin bubble and lift. The skin has also been pierced by the engraver, who has exposed the steel when cutting the initial on the handle. Impressed twice with 'Hutton', the maker's surname in full. (See Marks, page 216.) It is 11½in (29.2cm) long. £30-£50.

The Care of Close Plate

Little need be said at this point, if one heeds the warnings expressed above, avoiding both direct contact with heat, and over-exposure to water. Obviously one will have to wash close plate cutlery, if one wishes to use it, but this must be done carefully, to avoid fracturing the silver skin by knocking the pieces against one another. They should always be dried immediately afterwards with a soft cloth, and then be placed in a warm spot such as an airing cupboard, the heated atmosphere driving away any remaining moisture. Close plate should be stored in a dry, well-aired place. A damp atmosphere will inevitably cause great harm to the metal, while fluctuations in temperature may well split the ivory or bone handles, these materials eventually cracking if forced to expand and contract with temperature changes. Silver-cleaning creams can be used with impunity on pieces in good condition, while small patches of rust can be removed with fine wire wool, emery cloth, or even a damp cork dipped into an abrasive scouring powder. You must take care not to rub the silver with any of these materials however, as this would cause the skin to lift, exposing still more of the base metal to the ravages of damp.

Old Sheffield Plate or Fused Plate

Fused plating is a process in which a thin sheet of silver is fused by heat to a much thicker copper ingot, the two metals then reacting as one when hammered or rolled. Produced from the 1740s to the middle of the 19th. century, it is now more commonly known as Old Sheffield plate. This title is somewhat misleading, as vast quantities of fused plate were also manufactured in Birmingham, as well as in both France and Russia. Nevertheless the process was discovered by a Sheffield man, Thomas Boulsover, who was born in 1704 in Ecclesfield, a village some four miles from the present city centre. Regrettably there are only legends about his important find, the most commonly accepted stating that, in 1743, Boulsover was repairing a silver-cased copper knife handle. He accidentally overheated the two metals with his blow-pipe and, to his consternation, they fused together with a permanent bond. The second legend has it that Boulsover was working on a piece of metal held in a vice. This would not screw up tightly enough to secure the piece of metal, so he wedged it in place using a copper penny and a silver sixpence. Once again he was too lavish with the heat, with the result that the two coins fused together.

In fact the accident of fusing the two metals together is, perhaps, less important than Boulsover's experiments with the resultant sandwich of silver and copper. He discovered that, under pressure, the two metals acted as one, both expanding in total unison. Boulsover was quick to realise the commercial possibilities of his find. He saw that objects could be fashioned which looked exactly like silver but at a fraction of the cost, thereby creating relatively inexpensive but impressive-looking pieces for the rapidly-expanding middle class market.

The Process of Manufacture

Having outlined the basic principle of fused plate above, we must now explore in more detail the intricacies of the manufacturing process. Various experiments were carried out on both the copper ingot and the silver skin, until the most workable alloys were found to be copper mixed with zinc and lead and silver mixed with copper, the latter to the sterling standard of 925 parts of silver to every thousand parts of metal. An ingot measuring about two and a half inches wide, eight inches long, and one and a half inches thick of the former alloy was cast and then filed until one surface was perfectly smooth. A sheet of silver only about one eighth of an inch thick was then cut to size to fit this surface. This too was smoothed down and then placed on top of the copper ingot, the two perfect surfaces brought together with great care to ensure that no dirt, grease or moisture was sandwiched between them. The two metals then had to be forced together to expel any air. In Boulsover's day this was done by hammering on to a lump of iron placed on top of the metals which spread the pressure and ensured that the thin skin of silver was not marred by hammer blows. Before long, however, hydraulic presses were in use.

The thin silver sheet was then protected by a copper plate covered with a solution of chalk, preventing the two from fusing together, and then the three pieces of metal were bound together with iron wire. The edges where the copper ingot and the silver came into contact were treated with a solution of borax and then the sandwich was placed inside a coke-fired furnace. These furnaces were quite primitive, and it was impossible to regulate the temperature with any degree of accuracy. Consequently, a skilled worker was employed to observe the ingot heat up through a hole in the furnace door, keeping careful watch for the silver to melt and 'weep', small droplets running down the sides of the copper ingot. Once this stage was reached the ingot was removed from the furnace and allowed to cool. After cooling it was cleaned with acid and scoured with sand and water. The copper and silver sandwich was now ready to be flattened out into a sheet of workable metal.

At first the ingots were hand-beaten into sheets, but by the 1760s hand-driven rollers were employed. These were later replaced by rolling mills driven by horses, or water or steam power. The thickness of the sheet of metal might vary tremendously, sturdy metal being necessary for the manufacture of large pieces such as trays and entrée dishes. On the other hand, weighted candlesticks, their bases filled with pitch to create a misleading impression of solidity, were often made from extremely thin metal, as were boxes and buttons.

Early fused plate was covered on only one side with silver. The exposed copper was generally concealed by a thin plating of tin, applied in a molten state after the surface to be plated was covered with sal-ammoniac and then heated. While still hot the surface was wiped with a piece of soft linen to smooth out the molten tin, leaving a white finish. The colour of the tin matched the silver much more closely than the redness of the copper, creating the impression that the object was fashioned entirely from precious metal.

By the 1760s, silver could be fused on to two sides of the copper ingot, this development doing away with the necessity for tinning. Nevertheless, tinning was still used until the mid-19th century on pieces where it was considered an unnecessary expense to cover both sides of the sheet with silver. This cheaper process was employed where the tinned surface would rarely be seen – on the undersides of trays, salvers, and chamber candlesticks, and inside domed meat dish covers or teapots and other vessels. Experiments were also carried out to see whether the copper ingot could be covered on all four sides with sheet silver. This proved impossible, as insufficient heat was conducted to the centre of the sandwich to raise the temperature of the copper ingot enough for fusion to take place.

The majority of fused plate was raised from flat sheet metal by hand, each piece being subjected to thousands of hammer blows before the desired shape was achieved. Holloware such as teapots and coffee pots were made in the same way from sheet metal curved into a cylinder, the two edges soldered together. Usually a dentilled or 'cramped' seam was employed, this providing greater strength as the solder had a larger area upon which to act. Borders of entrée dishes, plates and trays were generally raised up using a tool called a swage. This acted as a template, its two hinged parts moulding a regular shape along the edges with the help of numerous hammer blows. Many swages of different sizes and shapes were manufactured from hardened steel, creating a bewildering variety of border mouldings.

By the mid-19th century, almost at the end of the fused plate industry, it had become standard practice to turn the metal into shape on wooden forms or 'chucks' spun on lathes. The workmen would force the metal on to the chuck until it acquired the exact shape, using wooden or steel burnishing tools. The men had to exert constant and even pressure as the lathe turned at a high rate. This quicker, and therefore cheaper, process is thought to have been introduced in the 1820s. Thomas Nicholson, a fused plate manufacturer, wrote in 1850:

> "Much of late years is accomplished by turning with a burnish on pieces of wood formed for the purpose, some forty years ago never contemplated. I remember

being laughed at for such an attempt, but it has today become an important advantage..."

Whether raised by hand with hammering, or spun on a lathe, there was always the risk that some of the thin skin of silver might be removed to reveal the red tones of the copper beneath. Similar blemishes might also occur at an earlier stage in manufacture, after the silver-plated copper ingot was rolled under pressure, the silver skin splitting to reveal unsightly marks or scars. To overcome these problems a technique called French plating was introduced. Here a workman would clean the affected area, scraping it smooth to ensure that it was completely free from grease or dust. He would then heat up a leaf of beaten silver, burnishing it down on to the fault under great pressure. Whilst burnishing each leaf he would be heating up the next, thereby saving time, applying several layers until the blemish was completely covered and until the requisite thickness of silver was built up. Usually as few as three or four leaves were all that was needed to repair fused plate, although far more could be applied if desired. Unfortunately the leaves were rather unstable, becoming detached quite easily. As a result this technique was useful only for disguising faults in flat areas which were unlikely to be subjected to much wear. Certainly the process was not durable enough to conceal copper edges, as these were very likely to be knocked when the piece was in everyday use. Moreover, it could not be employed for applying cartouches for engraved crests or monograms as the sharp tools used by the engravers tended to dislodge or tear the thin silver leaves. The two problems outlined above will be discussed more fully in the next section of this work.

Problems and Techniques Associated with Fused Plate

Having mentioned 'tinning' as a means of concealing the copper on items plated on only one side with silver, the manufacturers of fused plate were also faced with the problem of hiding the edge of copper which would be quite apparent to anyone who examined a piece from close quarters. Obviously prospective purchasers of fused plate would be loath to advertise the fact that they could not afford solid silver, so the makers had to find a way around this problem. At first a narrow strip of plated copper was soldered back to back on to the border, the edge then tinned for concealment but, in about 1785, business partners Samuel Roberts and George Cadman introduced the use of plated wire, drawing a strip of fused plate through a series of holes decreasing in size until the requisite diameter was achieved. The last hole was even shaped, so that the wire was grooved on one side. This was then soldered on to the edge of the piece, the groove fitting snugly over the tell-tale copper. This technique proved to be a very efficient way of concealing the copper, and was obviously very popular with the clients. Some manufacturers of fused plate even went to the trouble and expense of stamping their wares: 'Silver Edges' or 'Silver Borders', thus advertising that their pieces were of somewhat better quality. Today the presence of a wire soldered to the rim of an object is a useful indication that the piece is made of fused plate. The wire can be seen quite easily, or can be felt by testing the edge with a fingernail.

In the late 1780s, decorative beaded or gadrooned borders became fashionable on silver wares. The makers of fused plate had to introduce these too, to keep up with the latest fashions, and so they developed a technique of stamping out thin strips of silver with hardened steel dies, the soft precious metal taking on the design in great detail. These silver strips were then filled with molten tin and lead solder to give them strength, and they were then applied to the rims of pieces. It was a standard practice to leave a narrow edge of silver protruding over the rim. This could be bent over and then soldered on to the underside of the piece, serving, once again, to conceal the tell-tale edge of copper. This method was somewhat cheaper than that described above, but could only be used for items with simple shapes and borders. More complicated pieces still required the application of fused plate wire to their rims. Once again, one can often feel the turned over edge of silver with a fingernail. Alternatively, one may well be able to see the dull, grey tin and lead solder showing through the thin silver mounts on pieces that have been somewhat over-cleaned.

After successfully manufacturing items with concealed copper edges for some forty years, Samuel Roberts took out a patent, in 1824, for a new method. This involved the application of a silver thread or wire on to the rim. This thread was then hammered flat, and the projecting rim was filed off. Finally the silver thread was burnished on to the silver skin of the object until the seam disappeared. This new process was designed so that no-one could distinguish between fused plate and silver, even if they were to examine the piece in minute detail.

The feet, knobs, and handles of fused plate objects were generally made from two die-stamped halves filled with tin and lead solder and then soldered together. Often both sides were made from thin silver, although the insides of feet were usually made from fused plate as this was slightly cheaper. Obviously the manufacturers felt that they could get away with this small saving in cost, as few people would think to look carefully at the insides of feet. Moreover, the backs of feet would presumably be subjected to less cleaning, so there was little risk of the silver skin wearing out to reveal the copper beneath.

The majority of early fused plate was left perfectly plain, but chased decoration became popular in the third quarter of the 18th century. The process of chasing involves indenting a design using various punches, ranging from tough, sturdy tools to create the main curves and lines, to more delicate ones for finer detail. The piece to be decorated was embedded into a surface of pitch which gave the strength necessary to resist the hammer blows. Items which were not protected in this way might well deform and buckle under the stress. Chased decoration did not pose a problem for the manufacturers of fused plate, as the metal was simply pushed and stretched into the various designs. No silver was removed from the surface by the tools, so there was no danger of the copper being revealed.

However, when bright-cut engraved decoration on silver became popular in the 1780s, the makers of fused plate were faced with a dilemma. Engraving is carried out using finely-pointed chisel-like tools which actually scoop out and remove part of the surface metal. Obviously this posed an immediate threat, as the copper was thus exposed, spoiling the deception that the piece in question was made of solid silver. The makers of fused plate avoided this at first by using a heavier coating of silver, sometimes depositing no less than 24 ounces of silver on to every eight pounds of copper. This was simply not practical, as the cost of producing such heavily-plated sheets of copper was enormous. These increased costs were avoided by soldering on silver bands and by inserting more heavily-plated shields or cartouches. Although these methods were far more time-consuming, labour was cheap, even if one considers that only the most skilled and experienced workmen could hope to carry out such delicate operations with any degree of success, concealing the soldered joints from the gaze of the discerning buyer. Needless to say, this extra work had to be paid for, and the increased costs were, inevitably, passed on to the purchaser. Most companies seem to have added on just under 25 per cent of the basic cost of an object for inserting a shield for the engraving of crests, coats of arms, or monograms. A similar charge was also made for the application of silver borders, as described above.

Around 1810, a new process was invented for the engraving of crests on to items of fused plate. Here a thin plate of pure silver was cut out and fastened on to the surface of an object using a strip of wire. This plate was heated until it turned a dull red, and the wire was then removed, the plate of silver now sticking to the surface. The workman would then burnish down the plate, rubbing it hard and with great care to ensure that no air was trapped. If any air was allowed to remain, the plate would buckle and blister necessitating a repeat of the whole process after the plate was pierced to allow the offending air bubble to escape. Once the plate was stuck on to the surface it was hammered until the two were perfectly level with each other. After being reheated and burnished, or 'rubbed in', once again the plate was hammered over for a final time using a small hammer covered with a soft cloth. This removed any marks or blisters.

'Rubbed in' shields can be seen very easily on pieces which have been allowed to tarnish, as pure silver was used for the plates. The surfaces into which they were rubbed were made of sterling, or 925 standard, silver. The two metals tarnish at different rates, the pure silver discolouring more quickly than the lower standard alloy.

If one can see a shield inset into an object, or a cartouche rubbed into its surface, then one can be sure that the piece is made of fused plate rather than of electroplate. In the latter process, described later, a crest or monogram or any decoration can be engraved before the piece is plated, ensuring an equal distribution of silver over the entire surface, including any engravings.

Mention has been made above of the use of fused plate wire or thread to disguise the tell-tale copper edges, but wire was also used in the manufacture of baskets, bonbon dishes, condiments and toast racks, or to make handles for cruets and bottle holders. At first the sheets of fused plate were soldered around brass wire but this method proved to be unsatisfactory, as the skin tended to split. From the late 1760s fused plate wire was made in the rolling mills, a thin strip of sterling silver being bent around a circular copper ingot about one inch in diameter. After fusion had taken place under the influence of heating in a furnace, the bar was drawn through a series of holes or 'whortles', these decreasing in size until wire of the requisite diameter was created.

In around 1780 a simpler method was discovered, in which a sheet of pure silver was burnished around a copper rod. Considerable care and pressure were needed to ensure that any air bubbles were excluded. The resulting silver-covered bar could then be stretched through whortles as described above. Wirework baskets and dishes first became popular in the 1780s, and continued to be manufactured well into the 19th century, later examples having applied die-stamped florid rococo borders and acanthus leaf handles. Earlier specimens were more simple, with delicate bead or gadroon rims.

Another form of decoration was piercing, reintroduced by workers in silver in the mid-1700s. Once again, fused plate manufacturers were obliged to follow the fashions set by their rivals working in precious metal, hand-sawing the intricate designs of arabesques, slats and roundels. This laborious method could never be successful with fused plate, as the fret-saws left ragged edges of metal exposing the copper. Filing to remove the rough, unsightly edges simply revealed even more copper, spoiling the effect and making the piece impossible to sell. To overcome this problem the manufacturers of fused plate introduced the fly punch machine, a large press into which hardened steel chisel-like tools were fitted. These were cast in various shapes to cut out corresponding decorative designs in the metal. The fused plate object was placed in position under the chisel, a matching 'bed' being secured underneath. When the chisel was punched down it cut through the sheet of fused plate, the bedding plate beneath preventing the silver skin from stretching out of shape. As the chisel cut through the metal it dragged the flexible silver skin with it, concealing the copper edges.

Some pierced pieces were quite simple, with narrow friezes of stamped out holes on their rims and domed bases. Others were extremely elaborate, dish rings and baskets entirely covered with piercing becoming very popular in the late 18th century. One might imagine that so much piercing could well weaken the object, and so piercing was often combined with chasing of flutes or floral and foliate designs. This worked on the same principle as corrugated cardboard, the chasing adding strength by bowing and stretching the metal. Piercing using fly punches soon proved to be very successful, as it was so much quicker and cheaper than the traditional hand-sawn method. As a result it was even adopted by workers in silver, spreading throughout the industry until hand-piercing became almost a thing of the past.

Steel dies had been used for stamping shapes and decoration for many years, the Sheffield metal workers using this method for the manufacture of knife handles from early times. It is hardly surprising that the process was used extensively in the fused plate industry, particularly from the 1770s, when improvements in the hardening and tempering of cast steel were made. Before this development softer steel dies were used, the decoration needing subsequent 'sharpening' by hand to create greater detail. It can be very difficult to differentiate between die-stamped and hand-chased decoration, particularly as so many better-quality pieces were stamped and then finished off by hand. Once the various shapes were stamped out, their protruding edges were trimmed and then they were sent off to the assembly shop where they were soldered together. Decorative borders and handles were made in the same way, usually from thin sheet silver rather than from fused plate. These were then filled with lead and tin solder before being fixed into position.

Early Old Sheffield Plate

Having discovered the fusion of copper and silver, along with the curious property of the combination, Boulsover borrowed money from a Mr Pegge of Beauchief Hall, a local worthy and land-owner, in order to expand his production. He was able to repay the loan, with interest, in less than a year, as he soon found that his wares were immensely popular. Frederick Bradbury reports the following conversation between Boulsover and Pegge, as recorded by candlestick-maker Charles Dixon:

> Pegge: Why, Thomas, thy trade must be as good as making money.
> Boulsover: Yes, sir; but it is a deal better than making money, for I can sell my buttons readily for a guinea a dozen, and the silver does not cost more than 3s. a dozen: so it costs more to make money than they do.

From this one can see that Boulsover was manufacturing small items such as buttons, using thinly-rolled sheets of fused plate. Fused plate buttons continued to be made until the late 19th century. Indeed Bradbury states that, at the time of writing in 1912, "copper-plated buttons for uniforms and liveries are as extensively made of fused plated metal today as ever previously… Buttons plated by electro deposition cannot stand the hard wear and tear of actual use". While some buttons were die-stamped with arabesques or other patterns, the majority were embellished with family or military crests. Often employed for servants' uniforms, they must have been in common usage, judging from the number which still survive today. Single examples can still be bought very cheaply, although complete sets with both large buttons and

Five various unmarked mid-18th century livery buttons, die-stamped with crests, an armorial and a monogram. The central example was not cut out of its oblong plate to be finished off with a back plate and hanging loop. £10-20 each.

Photo courtesy David Sier,
Weston Park Museum, Sheffield

25

A later 2¾in (7cm) snuff box. This one has a hinged lid and has lead-filled, applied stamped silver ornaments, c.1810. £150-£200.

smaller ones for collars and cuffs may retail for several hundreds of pounds. It is worthwhile to look through the trays of junk jewellery which can often be found at flea markets and car boot sales. Here you may find the odd fused plate button which has been converted to a brooch by the addition of a simple pin and catch.

Boulsover is also thought to have made numerous small boxes, usually designed to hold snuff, although tiny patch and coin boxes were also produced in large quantities. The majority had simple pull-off lids, although hinged examples are not unknown. While some were hand-chased most were decorated with stamped designs cut into hardened steel dies, the latter also often used to decorate pocket watch cases. Elaborate rococo scrolls and foliage were popular in the mid-18th

Impossible to price, this saucepan is the earliest known piece of identifiably marked Old Sheffield plate. Formerly in the collection of Frederick Bradbury, and made by Joseph Hancock c.1755, it is fully marked on the handle mount. Crudely but sturdily constructed, the handle riveted to the copper body lined with silver, it has an overall length of 10in (25.4cm). Photo courtesy David Sier, Weston Park Museum, Sheffield

century, the exuberant and fanciful arabesques often incorporating classical or biblical figures. Although most are now badly worn with years of handling, one can sometimes make out the scene – a popular subject appears to have been The Judgement of Solomon. Usually the bottoms of these boxes were similarly decorated, generally with a smaller motif. Other boxes had lids inset with carved or engine-turned tortoiseshell, glass, or South Staffordshire enamel plaques painted with charming polychrome vignettes of flowers and birds. Many were applied with pierced fused plate mounts, the metal contrasting most effectively with the brightly-coloured glass or the rich brown tones of the tortoiseshell beneath.

The majority of boxes were made of sheets of copper coated on only one side with silver. Interiors were rarely tinned, and so all the seams and solder marks can be seen quite easily. Although vast quantities were made, it is now difficult to find specimens in good condition. Perfect examples would retail for £400-600 if correctly identified, although I have seen unascribed fused plate boxes in antique fairs for as little as £40-70.

Although snuff and other boxes were still made in Sheffield for many years, their importance within the fused plate industry gradually lessened. A directory of the town's trades produced in 1774 still listed many box-makers, but by now this section of the industry had been taken over to a large extent by the jewellers of Birmingham. The latter made hundreds of thousands of small boxes in both silver and fused plate, mass-producing them very cheaply and eventually putting the Sheffield box-makers out of business.

Thomas Boulsover's important discovery was soon to be eclipsed as he made so little use of his find, branching out into other industries and neglecting to exploit fused plate to its maximum potential. Another Sheffield man, Joseph Hancock, born around 1711, began to manufacture larger pieces of plate. Bradbury quotes the Reverend Edward Goodwin, in the introduction to *The Directory of Trades* mentioned above:

> "Buttons of brass or copper plated with silver were made by Mr. T. Boulsover about 50 years ago. But about 1758 a manufactory of this composition was begun

A mid-18th century hot water jug with wicker-covered handle and hand-chased gadroon decoration to the cover. The finial was die-stamped in two halves, which were then filled with lead solder. Notice the punches stamped on to the neck. Their size and position would lead the unwary to think that the jug was made of silver. 11½in (29.2cm) high. £300-£400.
Photo courtesy David Sier, Weston Park Museum, Sheffield

by Mr. Joseph Hancock, an ingenious mechanic, upon a more extensive scale, comprehending a great variety of articles, such as tea-urns, coffee-pots, saucepans, tankards, cups, candlesticks etc. etc. Since that time this branch has been pursued by various companies to great advantage, which has greatly contributed to the wealth and population of the town."

Regrettably very little is known of Hancock's history. He has often been said to have been one of Boulsover's apprentices, who disappeared with the secret of fusion of silver and copper after learning all that he could from the discoverer of the process. In fact, two Joseph Hancocks have been found in the relevant lists of apprentices, neither of whom ever worked for Boulsover. Despite the mystery of his origins, we do know that Hancock became Master Cutler of Sheffield from 1763-64, and was also one of the thirty original Guardians of the Sheffield Assay Office set up under Act of Parliament in 1773. He continued in this role until his death in 1791. His contemporaries were rather dismissive of Boulsover's contribution to the fused plate industry, praising Hancock as "the founder of the plated business in Sheffield, as he was the first person who commenced a manufactory of the goods". This appeared in a Sheffield newspaper report of his death. In a later work entitled 'Peak Scenery', published in 1818, the author, Ebenezer Rhodes, wrote:

"About the year 1750 a Mr. Joseph Hancock discovered, or rather, recovered, the art of covering ingots of copper with plated silver, which were afterwards flatted under rollers, and manufactured into a variety of articles in imitation of wrought silver plate. This business he introduced into the town of Sheffield, where it has since become one of its most important and lucrative concerns. Birmingham has attempted to rival this elegant manufacture, but, with the exception of the Soho establishment, its pretensions are humble."

It should be noted that "wrought silver plate" actually means solid, sterling silver, the old term "plate" describes articles made of the precious metal. "The Soho establishment" was that of Matthew Boulton, one of the most prolific makers of fused plate.

The above quotation implies that the secret of manufacturing fused plate was lost for a while, before being re-discovered by Hancock. This is unlikely to be the case and it now seems likely that Rhodes gave too much importance to Hancock. Nevertheless, the latter certainly did exploit the new material to a much greater extent that Boulsover. Dixon, the above-mentioned candlestick-maker, wrote:

"Mr. Joseph Hancock, in the year 1751, being a person possessed of a small capital, and a man of genious and an enterprising mind, was the first person who made any practical improvement in the use of silver-plated metal. He it was that led the way from the button to the candelabra, the plateau, the epergne, the splendid cup etc. Thus it is seen from small beginnings one of the most popular trades in the town and the kingdom had its origin, and the progressive improvements made in it are astonishing."

Hancock's first wares were plated on one side only, and were raised from flat sheet metal by hammering. The thickness of silver on the copper was far greater than one would find in later pieces. Hancock went on to the manufacture of pieces plated on both sides, and also pioneered the use of die stamps to make items such as candlesticks, their component parts stamped with various designs and then assembled with silver solder. Hancock's success led to others entering the field. As Dixon reported, "several firms began business and were chiefly formed of men of respectability, integrity and perseverance... There was great competition amongst them which house could produce the best articles and the cheapest."

Some of Hancock's pieces were marked in full with a stamp:

IOSH. HANCOCK

SHEFFIELD

Examples are now very rare however, and are much sought after by collectors of fused plate. Occasionally one may come across items impressed with the initials I.H. These pieces are contemporary with the output of Joseph Hancock, and may well have come from his workshop.

The Later Wares

Once the industry was well established, by the third quarter of the 18th century, Old Sheffield plate was used to produce an enormous selection of wares, ranging from vast, ostentatious centrepieces and tureens to more humble cups and flatware. Bradbury reproduces an extensive list of objects, taken from the earliest *Sheffield Directory* published in 1774, quoting, as follows:

> "These ingenious workmen make a great variety of articles, an account of which, here, may not be improper, viz.: epergnes, tea urns, coffee and tea pots, tea kettles and lamps, tankards and measures of all sizes, jugs, cups, goblets, tumblers, candlesticks, branches, cruet frames, water and platter plates, and dishes, dish rims, crosses, castors, tea trays, water bottles and writing stands, tureens, ladles, spoons, scallop shells, canisters, mustard pots round and oval, salts, bottle labels, cream pails, bread and sugar baskets, argyles, snuffer stands and dishes, wine funnels, skewers, cream jugs, lemon strainers, cheese toasters, chocolate pots, sauce pans, stew ditto, snuff boxes, bridle bits, stirrups, buckles, spurs, knife and fork handles, buttons for saddles, and a great variety of other articles."

Although this list seems exhaustingly comprehensive, a further *Directory* of the city, published in 1787, adds still more, introducing communion sets, entrée dishes, and decanter stands or coasters.

Not content with producing a huge assortment of pieces, the enterprising plate manufacturers also made an enormous range of designs within many of the categories listed above, thus satisfying the demands of a sophisticated buying public, who insisted on fashionable wares in this cheaper medium. Thus, Bradbury gives us a complete list of the products of the firm of Watson and Bradbury between 1788 and 1815, this single company producing no fewer than 217 candlestick designs as well as 111 chamber candlesticks and 182 'patent' candlesticks, 146 'bread basketts', 328 'liquor frames', and 269 epergnes. Needless to say, other pieces were made in far fewer styles, and this particular firm manufactured asparagus tongs, chocolate pots, chalices (presumably large pieces, for church use, as 19 patterns of goblets were also produced for every day drinking purposes), honey hives, marrow spoons, plate warmers, services, tea bells, toasting forks, tobacco boxes, and wine tasters, each with only one design.

One can argue that everything made in silver was also made in Old Sheffield plate, although the less expensive medium was used, perhaps, more for larger pieces. Here there was a much greater saving, as a great part of the cost of massive silver objects could be accounted for by the sheer weight of precious metal used in their manufacture. Skilled labour was still relatively cheap, so the makers of fused plate gained a real advantage over silversmiths, as they could make similar pieces using a fraction of the expensive silver which their rivals employed. The industry gained an even greater advantage in 1784, when a duty on silver was introduced by the government of Britain. This duty gradually increased, until silversmiths eventually had to pass on a rise in price of some 25 per cent to their customers. Obviously more and more people turned to fused plate to supply their needs, and there was a steady increase in both output, and in the number of firms manufacturing Old Sheffield plate. These advantages were overshadowed, to a large extent, when small items like cutlery were made. Here, the costs of labour in manufacture, and the preventative measures needed to ensure a long life, outweighed the savings in both cost of silver and tax. As a result, such minor pieces are comparatively rare, although their scarcity does not necessarily imply that they are very costly. One may still find small pieces such as sugar tongs or spoons for a few pounds if one is prepared to search around in junk shops and flea markets, as the majority of modern buyers are looking for large and impressive pieces, rather than for relatively insignificant curiosities.

It is interesting to note that the use of Old Sheffield plate was not limited to those on smaller incomes. One can still find many pieces bearing the armorials and crests of the wealthy nobility, who were quick to exploit this newly-invented material. They purchased many of the more imposing items such as centrepieces with their accompanying mirror plateaux, wine coolers, and massive candelabra. One notable buyer was Horace Walpole, Fourth Earl of Orford, who wrote to a friend, in 1760: "As I went to Lord Stafford's I passed through Sheffield, which is one of the foulest towns in England, in the most charming situation.... One man there has discovered the art of plating copper with silver. I bought a pair of candlesticks for two guineas that are quite pretty".

However, perhaps the largest and most receptive sections of the public, particularly for the smaller and cheaper wares, were the minor aristocracy and the middle classes. The latter felt especially insecure in their new positions in society, and were almost desperate to prove their respectability with the purchase of large quantities of plate. Ever keen to ape their more wealthy neighbours, they were delighted to be able to buy pieces which, at a glance, were indistinguishable from solid silver. While a closer examination might well reveal the lack of hallmarks, one would imagine that few friends or acquaintances would be impolite enough to scrutinize their host's 'silverware'. Indeed, only the collector of antique pieces really cares about the marks on his purchases. The contemporary buyer of Georgian silver paid little attention to such niceties as clear and well-defined stamps, and one finds, all too often, that the marks on antique silver have been rubbed away by years of over-zealous cleaning. Moreover, many pieces of early Old Sheffield plate were marked, using stamps which closely resembled those on contemporary silver. This caused a great deal of anger within the silver trade, as we will see later. Consequently the middle classes were able to deck their tables and sideboards with large displays of Old Sheffield plate, spending far less than if they were obliged to buy sterling silver.

While it would be impossible to describe every design of Old Sheffield plate made during the 18th and 19th centuries, I will attempt to outline the major developments in style in both form and decoration, by considering the main output of the fused plate industry. Finally, I will describe some of the rarities which one may be fortunate enough to find.

Candlesticks and Candelabra

If one adds together the various lighting devices in the pattern books of Watson and Bradbury, one arrives at the grand total of no fewer than 1,123 different designs. This seems a staggering figure, but one must bear in mind that houses relied almost entirely on candlelight throughout the 18th century and well into the 19th century. It is thought that candlesticks were one of the earliest products of the industry, and Bradbury illustrates two examples dating from the mid-18th century, one apparently struck with initials I.H., for Joseph Hancock, the other with script initials H.T. & Co., for Tudor and Leader. Both reproduce their silver contemporaries to the last detail,

A set of four of the earliest type of candlesticks to be made in Old Sheffield plate, dated c.1760. The hexagonal bases with moulded shells and the baluster stems have all been struck in steel dies. Die-stamping has not yet arrived. This set, 9¾in (24.8cm) high, is complete with Tudor and Leader's early mark on the nozzles, and is a very scarce item. £1,800-£2,200.

and are made of die-stamped sections soldered together, solidity and strength ensured by the insertion of an iron rod which passes through the stem up into the candle socket. Tall table candlesticks continued to be made in this way, the majority further strengthened by the addition of molten resin. This was poured into the bases of the sticks and then allowed to cool and harden, forming a solid, heavy mass. Candlesticks destined for the export market were often filled with a composition of plaster of Paris instead of pitch, as the latter might well melt in a hot climate. Finally, their bases were covered with baize, concealing the filling and also preventing the metal foot rim from scratching polished surfaces.

By the late 1760s neo-classical designs for candlesticks prevailed, with fluted columns and Corinthian, Doric and Ionic capitals. The bases were usually square, with simple die-stamped gadroon or bead decoration, although many examples were also enlivened with acanthus leaf or shell corners. Gradually designs became less severe, although the manufacturers rarely lost sight of the neo-classical motives. By the 1780s rams' heads and classical figures were introduced, along with floral swags, paterae, and urns. These relatively simple shapes were generally struck directly into the fused plate with hardened steel dies, the soft sheet metal reproducing the decoration in sharp, clear detail. At the same time candlesticks with lyre-shaped stems were made in large quantities, their stems manufactured from fused plate wire, now produced on a large scale. Oval bases were preferred at this time, often stamped with 'bat-wing' fluting, a decorative device which also served to strengthen the thin metal. This was usually repeated on the sconce.

The beginning of the 19th century saw the severity of the neo-classical fall into disfavour. The public now demanded more exuberant designs in both shape and decoration, so more elaborate candlesticks were soon produced, with baluster stems and shaped circular or oblong bases. Many were covered with a mass of rococo scrolling flowers and foliage, or with well-defined shells and gadrooning. It was impossible to simply die-stamp this type of heavy decoration, so mounts were made from stamped sheet silver, filled from the back with solder and then soldered

A set of four George III candlesticks with simple, elegant reeded decoration. Seams can be seen running up the stems and sockets. Made from thin metal, they are strengthened with steel rods and composition bases, the latter covered with baize. Unmarked, c.1780. £700-£1,000. In the centre we see an unmarked Victorian electroplated bottle stand with rim fashioned as a picket fence, the unusual motif repeated on the angled feet. Fitted with the original cut-glass decanters, it is 13½in (34.3cm) high. £600-£800.

A pair of candelabra with unusually elegant branches, and a pair of candlesticks, both c.1790, and with similar fluted decoration. The former, 19½in (49.5cm) high, would sell well at £700-£1,000, despite the fact that one has lost part of its finial, while the latter, one with missing nozzle, would retail for £250-£350. They are flanking a Regency centrepiece of c.1815, with original cut-glass bowl. Applied with die-stamped, solder-filled silver mounts and 16½in (41.9cm) tall, this would sell for £500-£700. All of these pieces are unmarked.

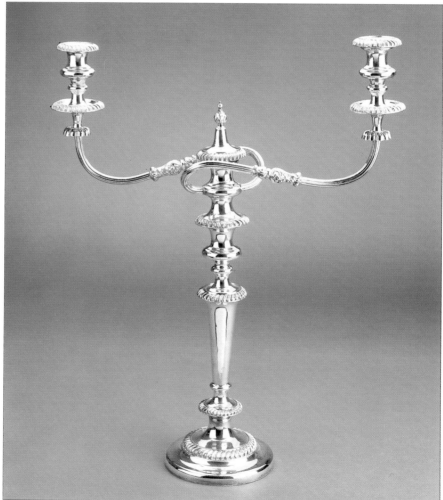

This page and facing page: *A suite of candelabra typical of those supplied to the wealthy of the first quarter of the 19th century, their large size and opulent decoration combining to create a splendid display.*

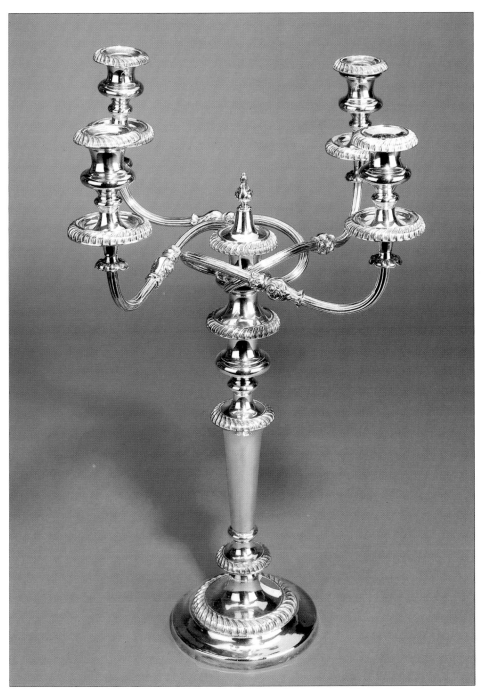

Moreover, this set of four Old Sheffield plate candlesticks, unmarked, c.1820, is very adaptable, as they were supplied with both three- and five-light tops, giving a total height of 22in. (55.9cm). £3,500-£4,500.

Two pairs of neo-classical candlesticks with drawn wire lyre-shaped stems, the tallest pair 12in (30.5cm) high. Dating to the last quarter of the 18th century, this design is popular if in good condition. Sadly, one of the larger pair has a replacement reeded nozzle, while one of the smaller pair is marred with several lead solder repairs. Their prices might therefore be reduced to £250-£350 per pair.

Moulded with vertical flutes and stylised palm leaves, this pair of unmarked 17in (43.2cm) two-light candelabra was made c.1780. A good size for a small dining room, but with some copper showing, they would retail for £600-£800, this price reflecting the slightly imperfect condition.

into place on the base, stem or sconce. Close examination of such pieces may well reveal that the silver mounts have worn away to some extent, exposing the dull, grey solder beneath.

The 19th century also saw the large-scale introduction of the telescopic candlestick, the stem sliding up and down so that the height could be adjusted. This clever invention meant that one could use the same sticks, fully extended on the sideboard or mantelpiece, to throw light over the whole room, and then reduce them in height for intimate dining or for close work such as sewing. The earliest telescopic candlesticks were introduced in the mid-1790s, using an ingenious interior mechanism patented by A. J. Eckhardt. Other makers soon followed suit with slightly differing mechanisms, many stamping their wares with their surname in full along with 'Patent'. Telescopic candlesticks are usually decorated in a quite simple way, with the addition of applied gadrooning and shells. They continued in manufacture until the late 1820s, the designs changing little over this period of almost forty years. Enormous quantities of Old Sheffield plate telescopic candlesticks must have been made, judging from the large numbers which still

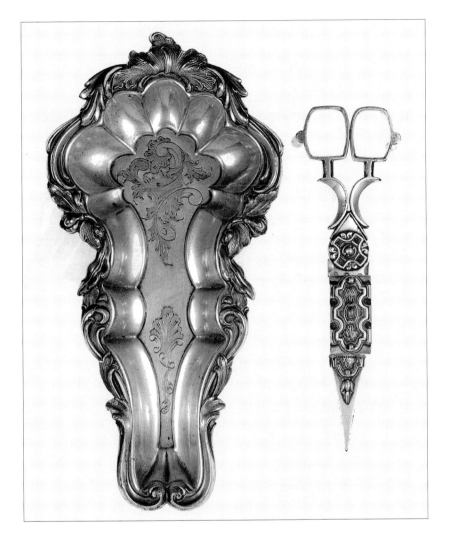

A late piece of fused plate impressed 'Mapplebeck & Lowe, January 27, 1840', applied with an elaborate solder-filled bud and leaf border, and with chased rococo decoration. This shape of snuffers' tray is most unusual and very desirable, hence £100-£150. 7¾in (19.7cm). It is illustrated with a pair of contemporary wick-trimmers applied with fused plate mounts and with close-plated steel blades and handles. Notice the bubbling surface of the crescent-shaped handle mount, caused by damp creeping beneath the silver skin. £50-£70.

remain today. Many are still in perfect working order, despite many years of use, although some specimens are now somewhat worn, their slide-action mechanisms loose and sloppy. Such pieces should be avoided, as they are very difficult to repair. Telescopic candlesticks in silver are, incidentally, extremely rare. One can perhaps assume that there was little need for them, as those people who could afford silver candlesticks probably had sufficient means to buy several pairs in different sizes, for their various needs.

Chamber candlesticks, designed to be carried upstairs to the bedrooms, were also made in huge quantities, particularly after the turn of the 18th century. These had large, flat bases for stability, applied with a rising handle, often fitted with a detachable snuffer. Many examples also had pierced short stems, the holes meant to hold pairs of wick-trimmers with steel blades. Although simple 18th century examples can still be found, they are now quite rare compared with their heavily ornate 19th century counterparts. These were applied with die-stamped borders, often incorporating trailing vines, a style of decoration which may seem inappropriate. However, there is a simple reason for this. To save the expense of making extra steel die stamps the enterprising manufacturers used those destined to produce the decoration on wine coasters, described further below.

One should look out for curious candlesticks with over large bases and sconces and shortened stems. These often appear strangely unbalanced, and one might well imagine that they have been cut down at some stage, perhaps because of damage. In fact these 'dwarf' candlesticks had a very specific use, implicit in their proper name, 'piano candlesticks'. They are extremely stable, as their weight is

A pair of unmarked Old Sheffield plate telescopic candlesticks made c.1815 and 10¼in (26cm) high when fully extended, each applied with die-stamped friezes of silver filled with lead solder. Although telescopic candlesticks are still readily available, it is difficult to find examples still in working order, most now with mechanisms too loose to support the socket with the candle in extended position. £250-£300.

Although chamber candlesticks in Old Sheffield plate can be found very easily, this example is unusual as it has a telescopic stem, here illustrated in the raised position. It is also complete, with the original wick-trimmers and conical snuffer. 6¼in (15.9cm) wide and unmarked, it dates to c.1815. £150-£200.

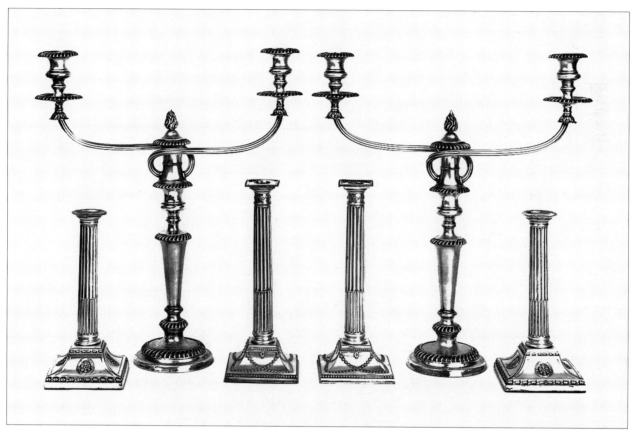

Two pairs of neo-classical weighted candlesticks die-stamped with paterae and swags, each still with its original nozzles with simple beaded borders. Made c.1775, they are in good condition, so might sell for £350-£450 per pair. The 22in (55.9cm) candelabra are rather later. Their solder-filled gadrooned mounts indicate a date c.1810, confirmed by the flame finials which replaced the earlier ball or vase-shaped finials. £700-£1,000. All of these pieces are unmarked.

A set of four of this rare form of candlestick is not often seen. These 11½in (29.2cm) caryatids provide a fine example of detailed moulding. Made about 1800, they are not every-one's idea of a beautiful style of candlestick, but they fetch a good price. £1,800-£2,200.

A set of four unmarked early 19th century candlesticks, two fitted with detachable candelabrum branches which increase their height to 18½in (45.7cm). The decoration is confined to simple gadrooning, indicating a date of c.1810. Sets of four are scarcer and more popular than pairs, so one could expect to pay £1,000-£1,500.

concentrated at the bottom and were designed to be placed on the top of pianos, casting light on to the sheet music and the keys. Their stability ensured that they stayed in place, refusing to topple over however spirited the pianist might be. Today they are very popular, as their reduced size makes them ideal for small rooms. They also make very useful desk furniture.

The styles of candelabra closely followed those of candlesticks, outlined above, although they were, of course, produced on a much larger scale. Early specimens were usually quite subdued, with only two or three sconces, but by the 1820s huge examples became popular, often with as many as six or eight sconces, and measuring between two and three feet high. Such pieces may be comparatively cheap, their huge size making them somewhat impractical in the modern home. Eighteenth century candelabra had simple drawn wire branches, often decorated with elegant reeding, but these soon developed into elaborate swirling leaves and flowers. This type of branch was made from two die-stamped halves strengthened with wire and filled with solder before being soldered together. Close inspection will usually reveal the lines of join, the silver solder used tarnishing more quickly than the fused plate. Many of these ornate pieces were supplied with similarly-decorated detachable finials, giving one the option of removing the central candle, while others have removable sections, enabling the height to be reduced by some six or eight inches. Some of the finest examples in this florid, ostentatious style were made by Matthew Boulton of Birmingham. His pieces were stamped with a double sunburst mark, usually on the side of the base. Throughout the 19th century many large silver candlesticks were supplied with Old Sheffield plate branches. This was presumably designed to cut costs, reducing the price quite considerably for the buyer.

A pair of early Old Sheffield plate candlesticks struck with facsimile hallmarks. Dating to c.1770 and 9¾in (24.8cm) high, they are in remarkably good condition, the small amount of 'bleeding' an attractive feature to most collectors. £500-£800.

An unmarked Old Sheffield plate 'storm' chamberstick, 8½in (21.6cm) high, with a tall glass chimney to protect the candle flame from a draught. Notice that it still has its conical extinguisher with wire handle, and that the sides are decorated with simple hand-pierced friezes. This piece dates to c.1780. £150-£200.

One of a pair of candlesticks applied with more elaborate acanthus leaf friezes and with campana-shaped sockets. 9in (22.9cm) high, and dating to c.1825, it is impressed with an unidentified maker's mark incorporating a sunburst similar to that used by Matthew Boulton. £120-£160 the pair.

Photo courtesy David Sier,
Weston Park Museum, Sheffield

One of a pair of unmarked 26in (66cm) candelabra showing the broad fluted decoration popular c.1825. Notice the seam which runs the length of the plain column. Although large and impressive, the design is somewhat poor, as the central socket does not match the two outer sockets. £500-£700.

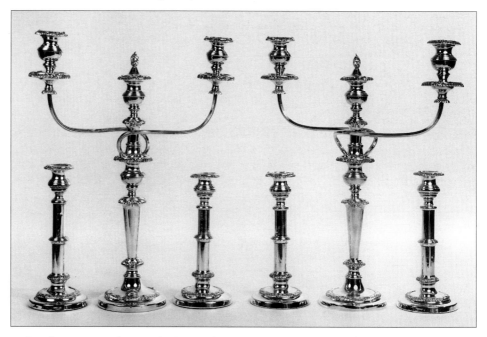

A handsome pair of unmarked 20in (50.8cm) candelabra with a set of four matching telescopic candlesticks, dating from the 1820s. The latter are illustrated in extended position, increasing their height from 8in (20.3cm) to 10in (25.4cm). Although all show some signs of 'bleeding', they are basically sound, with no serious damage or old repairs. It is rare to find such a complete set and one could pay as much as £2,000-£3,000.

By the early 1820s candelabra were becoming increasingly ornate, with applied gadroon, shell and foliate decoration. Their branches too were enhanced with die-stamped acanthus leaves. This 21in (53.3cm) pair was made by Matthew Boulton, a well-respected manufacturer, and bears his familiar double sunburst mark. £2,000-£3,000.

A similar pair of candelabra with unusual 'grenade' finials instead of the more common flame finials so popular in the first quarter of the 19th century. 19½in (49.5cm) tall, and engraved with contemporary armorials, they are unmarked. Nevertheless, they might sell for £800-£1,200.

The output of inexpensive candlesticks from Sheffield was enormous, and it is often difficult to ascribe individual pieces to specific makers. The steel dies, used both for forming the shapes and for then adding decoration, seem to have been somewhat interchangeable, certain manufacturers lending their equipment to their rivals from time to time. Moreover, it seems likely that a company such as Winter, Parsons and Hall, which specialised in candlesticks, sold much of its produce to other makers rather than directly to the public. There was nothing to prevent these 'retailers' from stamping the pieces with their own marks before they sold them, thus complicating the picture even further.

Finally, one may well be offered fused plate 'pen trays', small boat-shaped or rounded oblong trays about eight inches long. In fact, these are snuffers' trays, meant to hold pairs of candle wick-trimmers and conical snuffers. Huge numbers of these trays still survive so they are quite inexpensive, and one could buy an attractive example for as little as £40-60. Snuffers' trays with their original wick-trimmers are now difficult to find however, retailing for £100-150. They certainly make ideal pieces for desks, as they can hold paper clips, staples, and other odds and ends.

The makers of Old Sheffield plate made a number of pieces in drawn wire, usually dating from c.1790-1810. Here we see a 4¾in (12.1cm) wax-jack designed to hold a coil of sealing wax, along with a pair of wine coasters and a sugar bowl with cut glass liner. Notice that the rim of the bowl is applied with wire loops designed to hold a dozen teaspoons. All four pieces are unmarked. £300-£400, £400-£600 and £200-£250.

Another pair of extended 10¼in (26cm) telescopic candlesticks with applied shell decoration and with campana-shaped sockets, made c.1825. £250-£300. They are illustrated with an electro-plated satyr's head cigar lighter on a splendidly bold claw foot, c.1870, £200-£300, and with a curiously-shaped electroplated candlestick. Although the latter has a weighted base, it still looks unbalanced and rather ugly. It was presumably designed to cast light directly on to a book or piece of needlework. £150-£200.

An unmarked Old Sheffield plate wax jack made c.1820, the elaborate die-stamped silver border filled with lead, the 'frame' fashioned from plated wire. Only 5in (12.7cm) high, this charming piece would sell very well, especially if still fitted with the coiled coloured taper. See 'Writing Equipment' page 118. £300-£400.

As the 19th century progressed, candelabra became larger and more elaborate, the number of sockets often increasing to five or even more. This one of pair, made c.1830, is solidly-constructed and well-balanced. Just over 30in (76.2cm) tall and unmarked, they would retail for £3,000-£4,000.

This four-light candelabrum is lighter in both construction and appearance. Applied with a plenitude of die-stamped acanthus leaf decoration, and engraved with a contemporary armorial, it was probably originally one of a pair. 30in (76.2cm) tall and unmarked, it would now sell for £500-£700.

A rare 22½in (57.2cm) oil lamp with original fittings made c.1830, which illustrates well the exuberant floral and foliate decoration so popular in this era. Although damaged, and also spoiled to some extent as it has been converted to electricity, it might still sell for £1,200-£1,500. It is illustrated with a pair of unmarked electroplated lamp bases later fitted for electricity, £1,000-£1,200, and with an electroplated soup tureen and an electroplated venison dish and cover, both by Elkington and Co. The two latter items would sell for £400-£600 and for £600-£800 respectively.

This chamber candlestick, made by Blagdon, Hodgson and Co. of Sheffield, c.1825, still has its original nozzle, snuffer and wick-trimmers. Quite sophisticated, it is also fitted with a sliding ejector which pushes out the stub of a burnt candle. 6½in (16.5cm) wide overall, it would now sell for £150-£200 as it is so complete.

This unmarked 7½in (19cm) snuffers' tray was made c.1785. It has a simple reeded silver rim, and the centre is inset with a plaque designed to hold an engraved crest or monogram. Examples like this can still be found quite easily and cheaply. £40-£60.

Photo courtesy David Sier, Weston Park Museum, Sheffield

Dining Plate

Huge quantities of fused plate were made for the dining room, both for practical use and for display purposes. These range from simple, small pieces such as condiments to massive centrepieces and tureens, covering every style of silver popular during the 18th and 19th centuries.

The earliest salt cellars produced in this medium were of cauldron shape, their moulded circular bodies applied with gadrooned rims and die-stamped shell or hoof and scroll feet. Such pieces are now rare, as this design soon became unfashionable. By the 1770s salts were made from very thin metal decorated with hand-sawn piercing, this soon to be replaced by die-stamped piercing. Most were applied with gadroon or bead rims, these mounts serving to strengthen their somewhat flimsy bodies. The most popular shape at this time was the oval, although round and shaped oblong examples can still be found quite easily. Many were further decorated with stamped leaves or swags and paterae, and each was originally fitted with a glass liner, usually quite plain with the exception of a star-cut base. Although it is unusual to find an example with its original glass insert today, replacements can be made quite cheaply. Sadly the modern glass seems to lack the depth of colour of the original 'Bristol' blue or ruby glass. By the 1780s the claw and ball feet, made from two pieces of die-stamped metal filled with solder and then joined together, started to disappear, being replaced with simple, elegant curved legs with shell toes. Pedestal salt cellars with rising oval or hexafoil bases became popular at the turn of the century, this style superseded in its turn by heavier and clumsier oblong salts, their rims now applied with ornate shell and foliate decoration. By the end of the first decade of the 19th century, even the humble salt had become far more ostentatious, thus conforming to the current fashion for lavish display. Most salt cellars were now much larger, with heavy cut clear glass salts supported by drawn wire stands fastened to gilt trays. These trays, usually oblong or round, were generally applied with elaborate border mounts stamped in great detail with flowers and foliage.

Mustard pots followed similar trends to salt cellars, and one can still find many pierced examples with delicate scroll handles and shell or scroll thumb-pieces. Plain circular or oval 'drum' mustard pots were also manufactured throughout the Old Sheffield plate era, their popularity never seeming to wane. One can often only date drum mustard pots by examining their details, a simple reed or bead rim suggesting an early date. Later examples were decorated more lavishly, in the manner of the salts described above. By 1810 heavier shapes were fashionable, including the barrel, the fluted campana, and the moulded oblong. Such pieces are, to my eye at least, somewhat less attractive than their earlier counterparts.

Early pepper pots and muffineers were almost always vase-shaped, their bodies once again decorated with piercing and engraved swags. These charming pieces were invariably very light, being made from thinly-rolled metal, and so it is difficult to find examples in good condition. Solid, gilt-lined pepper pots were introduced on a large scale at the turn of the 18th century. The vase shape was still popular, although ovoid pedestal examples were also made at this time. The manufacture of individual peppers almost ceased in the 19th century, due the increased demand for large and comprehensive cruets fitted with numerous bottles.

Cruets in fused plate were introduced in the late 1760s, their designs identical to those of contemporary silver cruets. Indeed, the majority were fitted with cut-glass bottles with hallmarked silver rather than with plated mounts and lids, enabling the collector to date his finds with rather more accuracy than usual. Early cruets were round, with pierced holders for the simply-cut, clear glass bottles. These holders were adapted with great success from contemporary wine coasters, described in more detail below, by the simple addition of claw and ball feet and central scroll handles, the latter screwing conveniently into the holes in the wooden bases which were designed to be fitted with cartouches. The bottles were held securely in place by a shaped plate, suspended halfway up the stem of the handle. By the 1780s, the increase in manufacture of fused plate wire led to new forms of cruet, with boat-shaped, oval or oblong bases raised on ball or scroll feet. The bases were fitted with wirework superstructures, the drawn wire shaped into circles to provide snug holders for the bottles. The latter were now often embellished with more elaborate

An attractive pair of tapersticks c.1770 with entwined husk pillars, by John Winter & Co. Height 6¼in (15.9cm). The bases are die-stamped with festoons. £400-£500. (See Writing Equipment, page 118.)

One of a very fine pair of salts made in the late 1760s and bearing the early, so-called simulated hallmarks of Richard Morton, registered in 1765 and used until 1773. They are, of course, raised from the flat sheet and have a very fine gadroon border applied to conceal the copper edge. The three feet are each made from four separate pieces of plated copper soldered together so as to give the exact appearance of a silver example. £150-£200.

Three various salt cellars dating, left to right, to c.1780, 1785 and 1765. The cauldron-shaped example and the pierced circular example both have die-stamped feet filled with solder, while the 4in (10.2cm) wirework specimen has a stamped oval base. All are unmarked. £40-£60 each, although one could triple this price if one found a pair of fused plate salt cellars.

Photo courtesy David Sier, Weston Park Museum, Sheffield

A pair of unmarked Regency 4½in (11.4cm) cut-glass salts on oblong stands with buffed over gadroon, shell and foliate rims. The glass bowls are supported on drawn wire frames and the interiors are mercury-gilt, protecting the metal if salt is spilled. The undersides of the bases even have tiny applied silver corner mounts, ensuring that the copper will not be revealed. £100-£150 the pair.

cutting, and plain, coloured glass condiment bottles also became fashionable at this time, some of the latter further decorated with gilt script names denoting their original contents. This style of cruet varied little until the Regency period, when tastes changed and the public began to demand increasingly ornate tableware. Large cruets were soon introduced to satisfy this demand, many fitted with ten or twelve various bottles and pickle jars. The enormous weight of glass, often deeply-

Three various unmarked mustard pots dating, left to right, to c.1790, 1780 and 1810. The two pierced neo-classical examples were both decorated using a fly-punch, the machine creating delicate, regular designs. The 3in (7.6cm) drum-shaped pot is further enhanced by the application of die-stamped drapery swags and goats' masks. The fluted oblong pot is unusual, as it has two scrolling wirework handles. This seems to upset the symmetry of the piece, creating a rather ugly outline. £120-£180 each.

Photo courtesy David Sier,
Weston Park Museum, Sheffield

An attractive cruet, the base adapted from a snuffers' tray design by the addition of die-stamped feet and a wirework frame and handle. The contemporary blue cut-glass bottles have silver collars hallmarked in 1793, while the labels are made of fused plate. 7in (17.8cm) long and very desirable as so complete, this piece might retail for £400-£500.

An impressively elaborate William IV cruet, the bottles with silver tops hallmarked in Sheffield in 1835. Applied with die-stamped vine and arabesque mounts, this unmarked 11in (27.9cm) piece is still in excellent condition. £400-£500.

cut with fluting and ribbing, meant that these cruets had to be very solid and well-constructed, with thick wire handles and with sturdy ball feet. Decoration became equally solid in appearance, and many were covered with heavy gadrooning, shells, and acanthus leaves. These designs were frequently repeated on their central handles, die-stamped in two halves and then soldered together. Such pieces can still be found quite easily, although one should always examine the bottles closely for chips and cracks. Many are now fitted with later, replacement bottles, usually recognisable as they have electroplated neck mounts and lids rather than silver ones, as described above.

The manufacturers of toast racks also took advantage of improvements in the making of fused plate wire, creating both simple and more elaborate pieces made almost entirely from delicate wire soldered together. Although toast racks, first made in the 1780s, are still quite common, few are now in good condition. Most are marred with clumsy blobs of lead solder repairing weak spots where the silver solder used by the manufacturers has finally given way. Folding or telescopic toast racks were first patented in 1807 by Samuel Roberts. Some examples simply folded in half, their bases hinged at the centre, while other, more complicated, designs could be pulled out or compressed like a concertina, so that more or less toast could be held. Both types are now scarce, and rather expensive. Toast racks seem to be ever popular, although few are still used on the dining table. Instead they grace our desks as letter racks, attracting high prices if in good order.

Early egg cruets were also made mostly of drawn wire, providing both the handle and the frame which held the spoons and the gilt-lined cups in place. The latter were generally quite simple but sturdy, with applied bead or gadroon rims. While some egg cruets held four or six cups, some particularly charming examples

One of the most attractive cruets to be found either in silver or Old Sheffield plate. Known as a breakfast cruet, it embodies all the more desirable features. 7in (17.8cm) high, it has grace, style and good overall balance and symmetry and dates to around 1790. The piercing and bright cutting are superb. £400-£600. The single coaster dates from around 1780 and is worth £80-£120.

A machine-pierced and wirework 8in (20.3cm) toast rack c.1780, with die-stamped claw and ball feet, and with an applied beaded rim mount. Although such pieces are not rare, it is unusual to find an example in such good condition, hence £200-£250. It is illustrated with a rare wirework sugar bowl, c.1780, with twelve contemporary Old English pattern teaspoons. Although the latter are worn almost down to copper, it is most unusual to find such a complete set. The bowl is still fitted with its original blue glass liner. £300-£400. Both pieces are unmarked.

Photo courtesy
David Sier, Weston Park
Museum, Sheffield

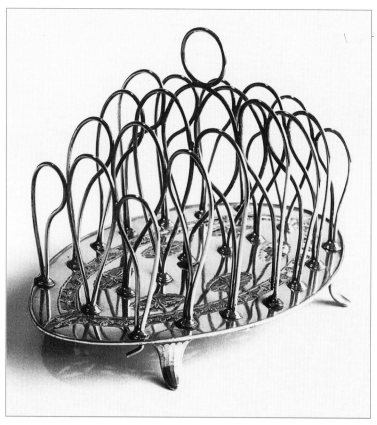

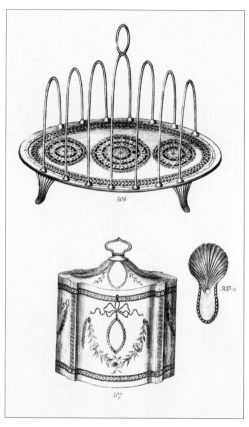

Another unmarked wirework toast rack with machine-pierced oval base, this example mounted on die-stamped fluted, curved feet. 7½in (19.1cm) long, and c.1790, it would retail for £150-£200.

A plate from a fused plate manufacturer's catalogue, illustrating a very similar toast rack, along with a chased tea caddy and a stamped out caddy spoon. Although the catalogue was not dated, one can assume from the designs of the pieces it illustrates that it was printed c.1790.

An unusual wirework telescopic toast rack with Gothic arch divisions and hollow ball feet. Unmarked, c.1810. £200-£300. It is illustrated with a pair of 9in (22.9cm) baluster candlesticks made c.1825, £250-£350, and with a pair of wine coasters applied with elaborate die-stamped rims. 6½in (16.5cm) in diameter and c.1825, these would sell for £300-£400. All these pieces are unmarked.

A sturdy beaded wirework egg cruet with die-stamped lions' mask and paw supports, dating to c.1810. 8½in (21.6cm) tall, and unmarked, it would retail today for £200-£300.

were made which held two egg cups as well as toast, these presumably designed for the solitary eater. Others held pepper pots or were fitted with salt cellars held just beneath the handle. By the Regency period egg cruets were much larger and less delicate. Both the stands and the cups were more floridly decorated, with stamped gadroon and shell mounts.

Fused plate egg boilers are very rare, so one may assume that few were made. They have round or oval bodies supported on stands over spirit lamps, the latter heating the water to cook the eggs which were suspended in the liquid in wirework frames. Although it has been argued that these strange objects were used simply to keep boiled eggs hot, this theory can be dismissed, as many egg boilers were fitted with tiny blown glass egg timers. This meant that the latecomer to the breakfast table could boil his eggs to his liking, instead of making do with hard, over-cooked eggs. Some of the more elaborate egg boilers were combined with egg cruets, although I have yet to see an example also fitted with condiments or a toast rack.

'Butter shells' in Old Sheffield plate can still be found, the majority perched on tiny stamped and applied periwinkle feet. Early examples were applied with beaded mounts, serving to conceal the tell-tale copper edges, while later specimens

A pair of large unmarked butter shells on die-stamped periwinkle feet. Notice the copper showing through the fluting and also on the engraved monograms. 5½in (14cm) long, these would sell for £150-£200 the pair.

generally had turned-over lips. Butter boats, smaller versions of sauce or gravy boats, were also popular for pouring melted butter onto asparagus. Their designs closely followed those of their larger counterparts, described below.

Bread, cake, fruit and bonbon baskets were made in profusion, again faithfully copying their silver cousins. 1760s and 1770s examples were hand-pierced with elaborate, flowing arabesques, shells and flowers, but by the latter part of the 18th century machine-piercing using a fly punch became increasingly common. Although the introduction of mechanisation led, in some cases, to more stilted,

An unmarked machine-pierced swing-handled cake or fruit basket dating from the last quarter of the 18th century. 11½in (29.2cm) long, its handle is applied with an oval silver cartouche designed to be engraved with a crest or monogram. £350-£450.

This unmarked basket, 10½in (26.7cm) in diameter, has a fluted foot and body, the flutes partly decorative but also serving to strengthen the metal. Chased with arabesques and with a die-stamped rim and swing handle, the centre has a presentation inscription dated 1825. £250-£350.

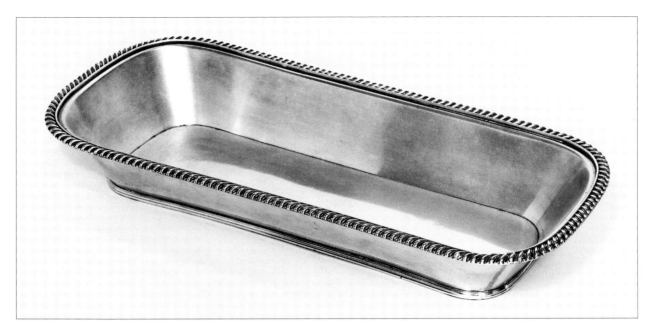

regular decoration, it is amazing how attractive and lively some of this later work can be. Punches of varying shapes were employed to great effect by the more skilled workers, who were able, in many cases, to create pieces which are almost impossible to tell from their hand-sawn counterparts. This elaborate decoration became unfashionable at the end of the century. Baskets were now pierced with friezes of regular slats incorporating paterae or roundels, although this more severe style was frequently enlivened by the addition of some engraved swags or vases of fruit. Once again, drawn wire was used from the 1780s until about 1815, the slender

An unmarked 12½in (31.7cm) knife or bread tray dating to the first quarter of the 19th century, the gadrooned silver rim burnished over to conceal the copper edge. Sturdy and attractive, these pieces are becoming popular, selling for £200-£300.

A very attractive example of a butter shell made by T. & J. Creswick c.1815. The shell and gadroon border is nicely executed and well proportioned. The shell border is edged with silver wire. The crest is the Baynes crest, Harefield Place, Middlesex. £70-£100.

Three soup tureens, the plain oblong 11½in (29.2cm) example dating from c.1810, the other two specimens from the second quarter of the 19th century. The earliest, most elegant piece might retail for £600-£800, but the other, more impressive tureens with their die-stamped mounts and handles, are more saleable, costing £1,000-£1,500 each.

This excellent unmarked 16in (40.6cm) soup tureen with matching sauce tureens was made around 1820. Bold in design, and with well-executed handles and acanthus leaf feet, such a set would prove very popular today. £2,500-£3,500.

A wonderful unmarked 22in (55.9cm) turtle soup tureen, finely engraved with an armorial and with realistically-chased 'scales'. The hinged 'shell' opens to reveal a detachable liner. Although Bradbury dates a similar piece to c.1795, I suspect it was probably made at the beginning of the 19th century. Such pieces rarely appear on the market, so one could expect to pay at least £7,000-£10,000 for an example in fine condition.

Photo courtesy of David Sier, Weston Park Museum, Sheffield

wires skilfully soldered on to a solid oblong or oval base, and then joined at the top by a thicker piece of wire. Seemingly frail and delicate, such pieces are surprisingly sturdy, quite a few surviving to grace our tables today. Later baskets are more solid and robust in appearance. Piercing became unfashionable, and by the 1820s fluted, shaped circular baskets had become popular. Many had applied rim mounts stamped with naturalistic fruit and foliage, their clumsy swing handles repeating this theme. Often rather ugly and vulgar, they still sell well today, perhaps because the earlier, more attractive type of basket is becoming increasingly scarce, and therefore more expensive.

Occasionally one may be lucky enough to find a gadrooned, or beaded, oblong, deep tray. About fifteen inches long, these were advertised in early 19th century catalogues as both 'bread' and 'cutlery' trays. Good examples are now quite rare, selling for £200-300.

Old Sheffield plate soup and sauce tureens were almost always large and imposing, serving to decorate the table as well as to keep their contents warm. Neo-classical vase-shaped specimens were covered with the standard motives described above, often with the addition of detailed goats' or rams' head handles and lovely artichoke or pineapple finials. By the early 19th century, however, rounded oblong or moulded oval tureens became popular. Raised on die-stamped rococo scroll or lions' paw feet and with applied scrolling foliate handles and melon finials, their bodies were usually left relatively plain. This showed off the elaborate mounts to full advantage. Body decoration was normally restricted to simple fluting, with the

A pair of unmarked 6½in (16.5cm) sauce tureens and covers dating to c.1815, with attractive dolphin handles and die-stamped solder-filled gadroon and shell mounts. Notice that the engraver has exposed the copper when he executed the crests. £600-£800.

A set of four slightly later 8½in (21.6cm) sauce tureens and covers made by T. and J. Creswick of Sheffield c.1825. These have rubbed-in cartouches so that crests can be engraved with no risk of exposing the copper. Attractively flamboyant, and with detailed stamped mounts, feet and handles, these could sell for £3,000-£5,000.

A good set of unmarked entrée dishes and covers, the handles detachable so that the covers can be reversed for use as extra dishes. Made c.1820 and 12½in (31.8cm) long, sets of four are always much more valuable than pairs, hence £2,000-£2,500.

addition of a gadrooned rim as a strengthening device. Perhaps the most commonly illustrated example of Old Sheffield plate is the soup tureen modelled as a turtle, its shape obviously denoting its contents. Twenty-two inches long, this splendid piece is a tour de force of the skill of the early 19th century craftsmen, with its realistic head and limbs and cover fashioned with scales. An example can be seen in Weston Park Museum, Sheffield, home of one of the best collections of fused plate in Britain.

Entrée dishes were frequently made en suite with tureens, their handles normally removable so that one could use the lid as an extra dish for holding cold food. Some were supplied with warming stands, the majority simply trays used to hold hot water, serving to keep the vegetables warm. Others, presumably more efficient, were fitted with spirit lamps, or had compartments designed to hold iron ingots which were heated in the oven prior to use. All are now very popular if in good condition, selling particularly well in pairs or sets of four. Single specimens can be bought much more cheaply however, and one could still buy a splendid specimen for £150-£200. Incidentally, it is quite common to find silver entrée dishes with fused plate warming stands; some particularly fine examples were made by Matthew Boulton in the 1820s and 1830s.

One might imagine that antique dealers would find massive oval meat dish covers rather hard to sell, as they are so difficult to display in the smaller home of today. Indeed, some few years ago they were in the doldrums, and many were cut in half to provide spurious 'antique' wall-hanging plant holders! Others were converted into more saleable tureens by the simple addition of scroll legs, although, of course, they were somewhat ineffectual as they did not have covers. Today, however, they have become much sought after, and one could pay many hundreds of pounds for a graduated set of five, the largest about two feet in diameter, the

A set of slightly later 14in (35.5cm) entrée dishes and covers with two-handled warming stands, each engraved with the arms of McGeough Bond of Drumshill, Northern Ireland. Made by James Waterhouse and Co. of Sheffield, c.1825, these would sell for £2,500-£3,500.

A pair of rather cumbersome 14in (35.6cm) entrée dishes and covers with warming stands with die-stamped decoration. Unmarked and c.1830, these would sell for £600-£800. They are illustrated with a Regency epergne, sadly lacking its original cut-glass bowls. Although replacements can be made, they are very expensive, so one could probably acquire this piece for as little as £300-£400.

Single entrée dishes are more difficult to sell than pairs or sets of four. This unmarked 11½in (29.2cm) example, made c.1825, has a clearly visible let-in shield engraved with two crests. £150-£200.

Another unmarked single entrée dish c.1825, with warming stand 13½in (34.3cm) diameter, and with die-stamped silver mounts. Notice that the engraver has made a mistake. He failed to line up the arms correctly with the centre of the let in shield, and so the end of the scroll cartouche has penetrated the silver skin of the lid, exposing the copper beneath. £150-£200.

A simple 20in (50.8cm) meat dish cover, once again with a let-in shield engraved with a crest. The tinned interior has an applied oval plaque to hold the screw-in handle, engraved: 'Best Sheffield Heavy Silver Plating'. (See Marks, page 217.) Made c.1820, this single example would retail for £200-£300.

A more elaborate 20in (50.8cm) meat dish cover applied with a frieze of die-stamped flowerheads. This example bears the crossed arrows mark of T. and J. Creswick (see page 217), and was made c.1830. £250-£350.

smallest perhaps twelve or fifteen inches. Extremely heavy, and with much ornate applied work, many are engraved with the armorials and crests of the aristocracy, showing that their use was not limited to middle class homes. Their interiors were usually tinned to avoid contact between the copper and the food, although some better quality examples were plated on both sides.

Plates, bowls and platters were made in large quantities, although only the latter can still be found with ease. One can, perhaps, assume that the former were subjected to more wear, eventually being discarded when worn until the copper was showing through the silver. Quite simple in design, most relied on a narrow band of beading or gadrooning on the rim for decoration. One useful invention was the plate stand, a shallow bowl designed to hold hot water so that one's dinner did not get cold during a leisurely meal. Still common today, these sell very cheaply as

Small objects in Old Sheffield plate are more difficult to find than larger examples, although their comparative rarity is seldom reflected in high prices. This delightful egg cruet, only 6¼in (15.9cm) high, is in remarkably good condition despite its fragile construction. Unmarked, it dates to the 1790s. £150-£200.

Meat dish covers were usually sold in sets of three or more. Here we have three from a set of five, the largest 18in (45.7cm) long. Applied with elaborate die-stamped friezes and with ornate handles, this unmarked set, made c.1825, would retail for £1,500-£2,000. They are illustrated with a pair of unmarked candelabra 21½in (54.6cm) high, made c.1830. Their branches are particularly attractive, hence a value of £800-£1,200.

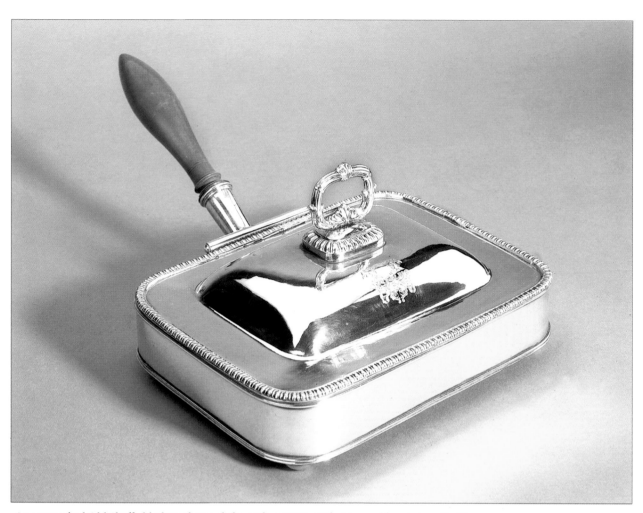

An unmarked Old Sheffield plate cheese dish made c.1800, with a turned beech handle. The lid is inset with a silver cartouche engraved with armorials, the use of the silver plate avoiding the exposure of copper by the engraver's tools. This example is 8¾in (22.2cm) wide. £250-£300.

A set of twelve unmarked 9in (22.9cm) dinner plates with simple applied gadroon borders, made in the first decade of the 19th century. Although odd plates can still be found quite easily, full sets of a dozen are now very scarce, hence £2,000-£3,000. They are illustrated with a pair of elegant candelabra made c.1790. Decorated with restrained stylised palm leaves, these would sell for £800-£1,200.

A typical dinner plate c.1820-30, 9¾in (24.8cm) diameter, with the added attraction of a hot water base. It is interesting to see that the hot water opening has been utilised for the application of a silver shield. On the opposite side is a normal rubbed-in shield, and both have been engraved. £80-£120.

matching plates of the correct size can rarely be found. Platters are always popular, especially if moulded with a gravy 'tree and well'. Usually fitted with a hot water chamber, these pieces are known in the silver trade as 'venison dishes'. A good example might well cost as much as £700-£1,000. Originally many sets of dishes were sold with an en suite mazarine, a pierced liner designed to hold the meat or fish, letting the cooking liquid drain away. Although very rare they are surprisingly inexpensive, and a good example sold for only £160 at a recent London auction.

Toasted cheese dishes, used for serving small pieces of rarebit as a savoury after the dessert, are also still quite cheap. Oblong or oval in shape, and once again fitted with a hot water chamber, they often contained a set of small dishes, each with an individual portion of the delicacy. Their hinged lids were removable, so that the cheese could be grilled until piping hot, the lid then attaching to the turned wooden handle with a fine chain so that one could pass the dish around with ease. Today they can still be found for as little as £250-£300.

Sauce boats again closely followed the fashions dictated by their silver counterparts, which also often had a great influence on contemporary porcelain shapes. Early examples were mounted on three shell and hoof feet and were rarely more than four inches long, but by the beginning of the 19th century the sauce boat had evolved into a much larger, more ostentatious piece, usually mounted on a domed oval base. The bodies were now chased with deep shell flutes, their rims were applied with broad scrolls, and the simple scroll handles of the 18th century were replaced by convoluted double and triple 'C' scroll handles stamped with foliage and with shell mounts. Today both styles are very expensive, although ironically one would have to pay more for a later, elaborate boat than one would for an elegantly simple 18th century example.

Argyles, small vessels designed to keep gravy hot by enclosing the liquid in a sheath containing boiling water, were manufactured in fused plate as well as in silver, the earliest dating to about 1765. Most closely resembled contemporary tea or coffee pots in form, the simple vase shape being particularly popular. The hot water was poured in through a small hinged flap, usually incorporated into the upper mount of the handle, and then the gravy was poured from a slender spout. These spouts were often let into the bottom of the pot, serving to exclude droplets of fat which might form on the surface of the gravy as it cooled. A rather ugly baluster shape was introduced at the end of the 18th century, this type with the scroll spout

A set of twelve 10½in (26.6cm) dinner plates made by T. and J. Creswick c.1830. These have more elaborate gadroon, shell and foliate rims. Although twenty or so years later than the previous examples they are more saleable, at £2,500-£3,500.

A handsome pair of venison dishes 22in (55.9cm) and 23in (58.4cm) long, with well-defined rims and with moulded gravy trees and wells. Made by James Waterhouse and Co. c.1835, and en suite with the entrée dishes on page 64, these imposing pieces always sell very well. £1,000-£1,500 the pair.

An unmarked machine-pierced 17½in (44.5cm) mazarine engraved with a crest which has revealed the copper beneath the thin silver skin. Designed to sit inside a platter, so that cooking fluids would drain away, mazarines are surprisingly inexpensive, despite their rarity. £200-£300.

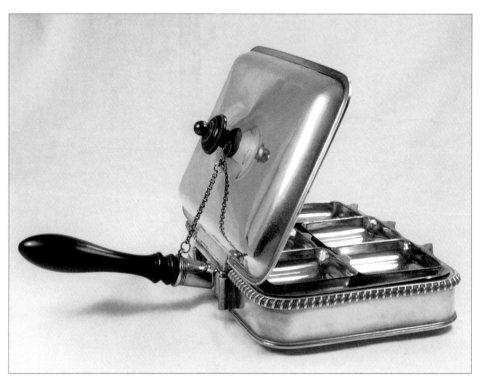

A cheese toaster of about 1800 made by Matthew Boulton, with a crisp gadrooned border to the dish. In this example the hot water is poured into the jacket through an opening in the handle socket formed by unscrewing the handle. 9in (22.9cm) by 6in (15.2cm). £250-£300.

An attractive unmarked 13in (33cm) toasted cheese dish with ebonised wood handle, the latter unscrewing so that hot water could be poured into the concealed reservoir. Circa 1815, this piece would cost £250-£350. It is illustrated with a late fused plate 9½in (24.1cm) coffee pot dating to the middle of the 19th century. The sturdy baluster shape is lightened by the foliate-stamped feet and scroll handle, and the piece is then finished off with a charming flower finial. £200-£300.

An early unmarked 5½in (14cm) Argyle with stamped gadroon decoration, made c.1770. The inner gravy compartment is surrounded by a hot water reservoir which acts as an insulator. Notice that the spout rises from the bottom of the pot, a common feature of most Argyles. This was to avoid pouring out the fat which would separate and rise to the surface as the gravy cooled. Although damaged, it is a very rare piece, hence £300-£400. It is illustrated with a contemporary inkstand with similar decoration. 9½in (24.1cm) long, this would also sell for £300-£400.

Another unmarked Argyle of baluster form, with a wicker-covered handle, c.1780. 6½in (16.5cm) high, this is, to my eye, an unattractive, ungainly piece. Nevertheless its rarity would again ensure a price of £300-£400. It is illustrated with a sauceboat with silver borders, probably made by Roberts, Cadman and Co., c.1825. 7in (17.8cm) long, it is similar to an example depicted in Bradbury's A History of Old Sheffield Plate. *£150-£200 for a single example, although a pair might sell for £700-£1,000.*

Photo courtesy David Sier, Weston Park Museum, Sheffield

An attractive Argyle decorated with beading. Notice the applied wire on the borders of the spout and the lid, concealing the tell-tale copper edges. c.1790 and 7in (17.8cm) tall, this would again realise £300-£400. Unmarked.

A rare, unmarked revolving epergne or centrepiece dating from the last quarter of the 18th century, fitted with a range of fruit and bonbon dishes and with hand-pierced galleries. The cylindrical wirework supports were presumably designed to hold vases or condiment bottles. These are now missing, and have been replaced with plain glass jars. Notice that the scalloped base has an applied silver wire to hide the copper edge. 23in (58.4cm) tall and made c.1780, one could expect to pay £6,000-£10,000 for such a scarce and attractive object.

set at right angles to the wooden handle. All argyles are now rare, and much sought after, so one could expect to pay at least £300-£400 for an early example in good condition. A later specimen dating from the 1820s might cost a little less, however, if one can tolerate the somewhat strange proportions.

Arguably one of the most impressive pieces of Old Sheffield plate was the supper set, a revolving stand fitted with a central soup tureen surrounded by three or four entrée dishes and several condiments. Two feet or more in diameter, complete specimens are now very rare and valuable, retailing for £4,000-£6,000. One must be aware of copies, often made in America, of electroplated copper, with crudely-moulded white 'vaseline' glass handles. Some are old enough to show signs of wear, revealing a tantalising glimpse of red metal beneath the thin silver outer skin. Closer examination, however, soon shows a distinct lack of quality, and one can see quite easily that the mounts are electroplated after soldering, rather than being made of die-stamped silver. I have seen such copies on offer in antique shops in both Britain and abroad, erroneously labelled as 'Old Sheffield Plate, circa 1810', often with prices approaching those one would expect to pay for the genuine article!

I will discuss other, more unusual, pieces of fused plate associated with the dining room in a later section, but now I come to the *pièce de résistance* of the sideboard or dining table, the epergne or centrepiece. Made almost purely for display, although many examples incorporate candle sconces and bonbon dishes, the silver epergne has enjoyed an extremely long history. Fused plate examples were first manufactured in the third quarter of the 18th century, using drawn wire for the delicately scrolling branches which were fitted with hand-pierced baskets.

This 18½in (47cm) unmarked Regency centrepiece has caryatid supports and very elaborate branches die-stamped with vines. Large and imposing, this would have looked splendid when covered with fruit and flowers. Notice that the candle sconces can be unscrewed, leaving behind circular bonbon dish holders. Sadly, all the glass and one of the nozzles are now missing, so the value is greatly reduced. £600-£800.

Another caryatid centrepiece, rather more attractive than the last, with a lighter base and with more delicate branches. The simulated basket-weave fruit bowl is particularly pleasing. 22in (55.9cm) tall, made by I. and I. Waterhouse and Co., c.1830. £1,000-£1,200.

This epergne, with original cut-glass bowls and with galleried mirror plateau, is illustrated in Bradbury's A History of Old Sheffield Plate. Made by Roberts, Cadman and Co., and dated to 1822 by Bradbury, it is 16½in (41.9cm) high. £2,000-£2,500.

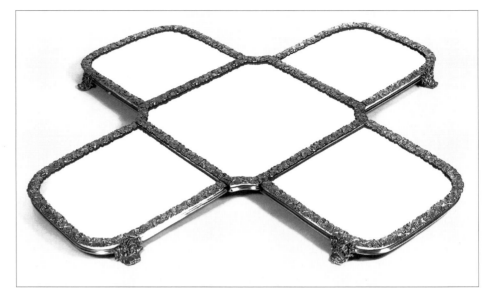

A rare, unmarked quatrefoil mirror plateau almost 50in (127cm) long, with a well-defined die-stamped vine border. c.1830, this could sell for as much as £3,000-£5,000.

An unmarked mid-19th century 19½in (49.5cm) epergne with shaped circular mirror plateau, photographed with alternating candle sconces and bonbon dishes. Splendidly ornate, and very popular today, this would retail for £2,000-£2,500.

These were filled with flowers, crystalised fruit, and other delicacies, adding colour to the table and also serving as part of the dessert. Many epergnes of this period were also fitted with cut-glass condiment bottles, creating a delightful, sparkling effect. Such early specimens are now, sadly, very rare, although one can still find numerous examples of early to mid-19th century centrepieces moulded in high relief with flowers and fruit. Most had a large central cut-glass fruit bowl surrounded by four or more matching bonbon dishes, each supported in a pierced holder borne aloft by an elaborate scrolling branch. All too often some, or all, of the bowls are missing or broken, the latter often clumsily repaired with steel rivets. Replacements can be made, but this would prove to be very expensive. The pierced bowl holders were frequently removable for ease of cleaning and storage, while many examples had candle sconces which could be screwed into place as an alternative to the bonbon dishes. Some of the most elaborate epergnes stood on detached stands or plateaux inset with mirror glass, which served to reflect the candlelight, thus enhancing the beauty of the arrangement. One might well imagine that such splendid pieces would be hard to sell today. Few of us live in such grand, spacious surroundings as our wealthy ancestors, so might find it difficult to display an epergne with plateau to its full advantage. In fact they find a ready market, invariably attracting high prices, if in good condition. A good centrepiece with original glass and mirror plateau could well sell for £1,000-£1,500 at auction, with a subsequent retail price approaching £3,000.

Cutlery

As I mentioned above, the manufacturers of Old Sheffield plate made relatively small amounts of cutlery, compared with their huge output of other wares. Presumably they found it more difficult to compete with the London makers of silver flatware, who used quite small amounts of silver to produce masses of machine-rolled sheet metal, stamped out into spoons and forks with comparatively little hand-work necessary to manufacture the finished product. Moreover, the repeated attempts at making fused plate flatware were never very successful. While a number of tiny teaspoons and sugar tongs were made from drawn wire beaten flat to form the handles and bowls, in the last quarter of the 18th century, these pieces inevitably wore out too quickly to appeal to the thrifty buyer, their silver skin proving too thin to withstand cleaning and everyday use. This period also saw the tremendous popularity of bright-cut engraving, a form of decoration which involves the removal of small lines of silver cut at an angle to create an attractive, sparkling effect. Especially fashionable on flatware, this method of enhancement was impossible to achieve on fused plate, as the engraver's tools removed the surface layer of silver to reveal the copper beneath. The same problem arose when customers wanted their monograms or crests engraved on to their flatware.

Obviously, cutlery in day to day use was also subjected to far more wear and tear than larger pieces, again resulting in the exposure of the copper. To overcome this problem, forks were made with tiny silver points soldered on to the tips of their prongs. The handles and shanks were manufactured from two die-stamped sheets of metal soldered together after being filled with an amalgam of tin and lead. One can see both the silver tips and the seams quite easily, especially if a piece is allowed to tarnish. Larger flatware items such as soup ladles and basting spoons were made in the same, labour-intensive, way. Relatively weak, due to the softness of their filling, few still survive today.

 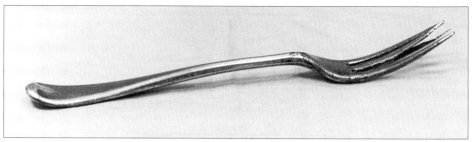

A three-pronged fork made in two sections soldered longitudinally and with silver tips soldered to each prong. The centre prong has split, showing very well how it had been originally joined. This also illustrates the sort of problem which confronted early platers. Late 18th century, £8-£12.

Three fish or pudding slices, the central 13in (33cm) example the earliest in date. Made c.1770, it has a hand-sawn pierced fused plate blade with delicate gadroon rim. The unmarked handle is made of thin sheet silver filled with pitch, to give greater strength. £300-£400. The two outer slices are somewhat later, dating from the last quarter of the 18th century. Both have machine-pierced blades. £200-£250 each. All are unmarked.

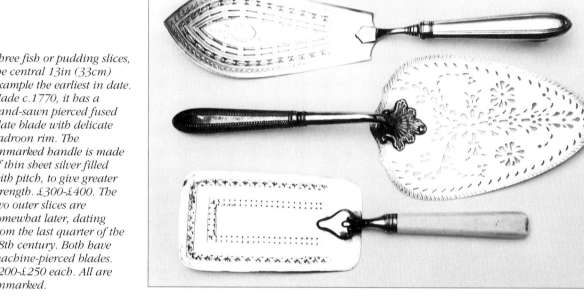

Other items of cutlery, such as caddy spoons and pastry and fish slices were made from flat sheet metal plated on both sides, the former die-stamped with attractive shell fluting to strengthen their flimsy bowls, the latter often hand-pierced with arabesques, shells, or rather naïve fishes or dolphins. Many slices were fitted with green-stained ivory or bone handles, sadly all too often now cracked after exposure to boiling water, or with hollow fused plate handles made in two halves soldered together and then weighted with pitch. This latter kind of handle was produced in large quantities for knives and forks with steel blades and prongs. Similar pieces were made for the consumption of dessert, although here the blades and prongs were usually close-plated, using the method described above.

Single, simple items of fused plate flatware can still be bought very cheaply, and one may be lucky enough to find the odd spoon or fork in a 'junk tray' for a couple of pounds. Larger pieces, such as ladles and serving spoons may cost £100-£200, while an attractive slice would be a bargain at this price. One could expect to pay up to £400 for one of the latter.

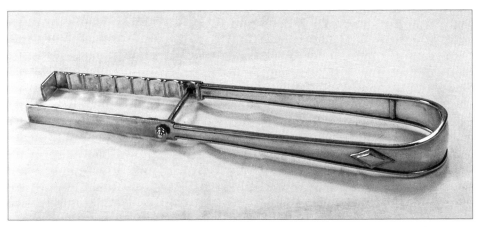

This pair of asparagus tongs is 10in (25.4cm) long and was made around 1800. The various sections are made up of single-side plated sheet soldered together to make a strong implement. The rounded border is formed by a strong silver wire edge. £150-£200.

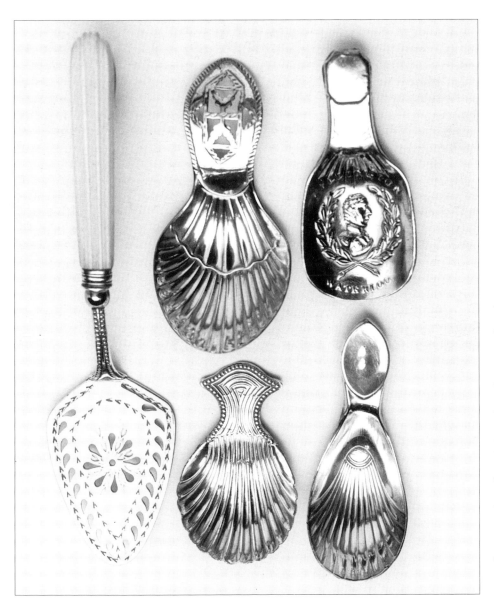

Four late 18th and early 19th century die-stamped caddy spoons, including a rare example decorated with the bust of the Duke of Wellington, made to commemorate the battle of Waterloo, in 1815. Caddy spoons with shell-fluted bowls are still commonly available for £40-£60, although the Wellington example might cost £150-£200. They are illustrated with a 7in (17.8cm) butter spade c.1780, with machine-pierced blade and carved mother-of-pearl handle. This would cost £100-£150. All are unmarked.

Old Sheffield plate wirework pieces are rarely in good condition today, their fragile nature ensuring that most examples are marred with solder repairs. Illustrated is an unmarked cake or fruit basket in pristine condition. 10½in (26.7cm) in diameter, it has a swing handle and a reeded foot rim. £300-£500.

Two examples of unmarked Old Sheffield plate, the 15½in (39.4cm) salver c.1790, the swing-handled cake basket c.1810. Both are plated on only one side, their undersides tinned to cover the copper, and both are inset with silver cartouches designed to contain engraved armorials or initials. £300-£500 each.

Tea and Coffee Accessories

As one might expect, the shapes of tea and coffee pots and their accoutrements closely followed those of their silver counterparts. They were among the first items to be manufactured in Old Sheffield plate, their bodies made from flat, sheet metal curved round and then soldered. One can easily detect the seam on early examples, particularly if they are allowed to tarnish. A line of silver solder appears, sometimes straight but more often castellated or dentilled, this shaping giving added strength, as the solder had a greater area upon which it could act. This solder line should also be visible on spouts and on handle mounts. Unfortunately tea and coffee wares were subjected to almost constant use, so all too often they are badly worn or damaged.

The first teapots, dating from the 1760s, were of a simple drum shape, with detachable rather than hinged lids, and with tapering, angular spouts. Most were applied with delicately scrolling fruitwood or ivory handles, now all too often broken or replaced. These small teapots were normally supplied with circular stands on claw and ball feet, the stands preventing the hot metal from marking the polished surface of the table. Occasionally one may find an octagonal example, but such pieces are now rare. Both types were usually left plain, although some were applied with friezes of tiny silver beads. It is curious that both the teapots and their stands were often engraved with crests or monograms. As they were made before the discovery of let-in or rubbed-in cartouches, this engraving inevitably exposed the copper.

By the mid-1770s, oval teapots became fashionable. Although their spouts, handles and stands were similar to those described above, most now had hinged lids with ivory button or pineapple finials. While some specimens were flat-chased with flutes or scrolls, many were now applied with narrow bands of silver, enabling

This attractive, unmarked 5½in (14cm) teapot with stand was made c.1780. Simple and elegant, it has a die-stamped spout and handle mounts, the solder lines still clearly visible. The cartouche is chased to avoid the exposure of the copper beneath the silver skin. The crest, however, is engraved, and so, inevitably, some silver is revealed. £350-£450 the two.

A 10in (25.4cm) baluster coffee pot dating to the third quarter of the 18th century, once again with die-stamped and soldered spout and handle mounts. This piece bears the traces of marks around the neck, obviously trying to copy silver hallmarks of the period. £300-£500.

A plate from an undated manufacturer's catalogue marked with initials T. L. and Co., probably for Thomas Law of Sheffield. This shows a hot water jug typical of the last quarter of the 18th century, with a simple vase shape enlivened with applied silver beaded bands and with a charming acorn finial. A similar piece might sell for £300-£500.

the engravers to add pleasantly restrained friezes of bright-cut flowers and foliage. At the turn of the century heavier, oblong forms were introduced, with scroll spouts and wooden bracket handles. Decoration became less subtle and, at the same time, the use of teapot stands ceased. Now teapots were perched on hollow ball feet, obviating the need for separate stands.

Teapot designs changed yet again around 1820, when a compressed, moulded circular shape became popular. Many were now die-stamped in two halves joined in the middle, a broad strip of reeded silver concealing the seam. Metal handles with bone or ivory insulating bands were now introduced, as were domed circular bases. Later still, many teapots were given die-stamped rococo rim mounts, this decoration echoed in the spouts and finials, which were stamped with elaborate scrolls and flowers. The moulded circular teapot continued to be fashionable until the mid-19th century, although some examples were slightly altered, their bodies heavily chased with melon fluting. One can still find a wide selection of later teapots priced between £100-£150, although a good early specimen could retail for £300-£400, making even more if still with its original stand. The latter are popular on their own, as they make useful small salvers, so one could expect to pay at least £100 for an attractive, perfect example.

In the 1760s, coffee pots and hot water jugs were of baluster form, often finely-chased with charming arabesques, and with gadrooned circular bases and domed covers. This type was soon superseded, however, by an elegant vase shape, totally in keeping with the current taste for the severe lines of the neo-classical.

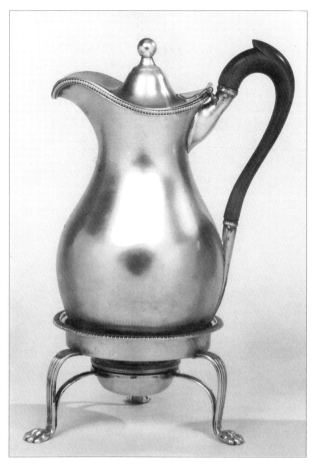

Above: *A nice example of a 7¾in (19.7cm) coffee jug c.1810. It is of baluster shape with a well proportioned spout and matching heater on paw feet, with a fine gadroon border to the rim. £400-£600.*

Above right: *A 10½in (26.6cm) hot water jug c.1805-10. The foot is the same shape as Adam period examples but the body is baluster shape. £300-£500.*

A sturdy three-piece teaset decorated with broad vertical flutes and with applied die-stamped foliate rims. Unmarked, and dating to c.1820, the teapot is 6½in (16.5cm) high. Notice that the milk jug has obviously been used more often than the other two pieces, as a lot of copper is bleeding through the silver skin on the fluting. These teasets are still readily available for £250-£300.

An unusually complete five-piece tea and coffee set with two teapots for Indian and China tea. This set has vacant rubbed-in circular cartouches and well defined die-stamped acanthus leaf rims. The bases are applied with drawn fused plate wires to cover up any exposed copper edges. Unmarked, and c.1830, the coffee pot is 9½in (24.1cm) tall. £2,000-£3,000.

An interesting transitional period 11½in (29.2cm) coffee pot, with fused plate body, spout and handle, but with electroplated feet and finial. Made in the 1850s and unmarked, it is a rare survivor. Although rather cumbersome in appearance, it would be of great interest to collectors, as it spans the period of conflict between fused plate and electroplate. £180-£220, despite the large dent.

An unmarked 14in (35.6cm) tea urn made c.1790, applied with silver bands decorated with bright-cut engraving, and with an applied silver cartouche finely engraved with drapery swags. The spout, ball feet and finial are made from die-stamped fused plate. Attractively small, this would retail for £700-£1,000. It is illustrated with two pairs of almost identical telescopic candlesticks. The seams on the stems and bases can be seen quite clearly on the pair at the back. £250-£300 per pair.

A pair of unmarked 10½in (26.7cm) 'globe' or 'balloon' tea urns made c.1800. Notice the silver wires soldered on to the joints of the square pedestal bases and on to the rims. Each urn is applied with a cartouche of fused plate made with a thicker coating of silver than was usual. Despite this precaution, some copper is still showing through the engraved initials. Pairs of urns are scarce, and these have the added attraction of small size and an unusual shape, hence £2,500-£3,500.

Above: *An unmarked Regency oblong urn on lions' paw and ball feet, applied with die-stamped geometric friezes and with rather unattractive carrying handles. 25½in (64.8cm) tall, it was made c.1815. £700-£1,000.*

A delightful tea urn of about 1780. Made by Thos. Law & Co., it has chased decoration, a shell finial and a very attractive dolphin spout. A further attraction is that it is not big, being only 14½in (36.8cm) high. This is the typical Adam shape of the period. £1,200-£1,500.

Gadrooning was generally replaced by beading, and many were also applied with silver bands, bright-cut or stamped with swags and paterae. Eighteenth century coffee pots were rarely sold en suite with tea services, so new shapes were able to evolve. These included the tapering cylinder, sometimes plain, sometimes chased, the inverted pear, and the 'beehive', the latter of ovoid form, chased with broad, horizontal flutes. All these very different shapes were fashionable from about 1785 until 1815. Fused plate coffee pots sell well, despite the fact that there are still numerous good examples on the market. Ever popular, they may make as much as £300-£400.

In the Regency period, the public began to demand matched tea and coffee sets, so the coffee pot was made to conform with the shapes of teapots described above. Complete sets are now very rare, retailing for £2,000-£3,000. An exception to the above rule was the coffee biggin, a cylindrical or barrel-shaped pot with squat spout. These were always sold with a stand fitted with a spirit burner. Simple and totally functional, these are very popular today, selling for £200-£300 if complete.

A somewhat later tea urn applied with die-stamped gadroon mounts, and with well-defined paw feet and scrolling foliate handles. The pineapple finial is particularly attractive. This 17in (43.2cm) piece was made by Matthew Boulton of Birmingham, c.1820, and bears the crest and armorial of Ralph Leycester of Toft, Cheshire, engraved on to a rubbed-in cartouche. Boulton is a great favourite of many collectors, as his work is generally of marvellous quality. £1,200-£1,500.

Tea urns, vessels which once graced the sideboard, enabling the lady of the house to replenish the teapot without summoning a servant, were made in all of the shapes described above. Eighteenth century examples were normally elegant and quite small, usually measuring no more than eighteen inches high. Most maintained the temperature of the water with the aid of an iron ingot, heated in the oven and then placed inside an internal waterproof cylindrical holder. By the turn of the century larger, more ostentatious designs were introduced, echoing the various fashionable teapot shapes. Simple scroll handles were replaced by florid die-stamped handles smothered with flowers and foliage, or by rather grotesque lions' masks with reeded ring drop handles, and the shell-carved ivory taps were surrounded by great swags of acanthus leaves. Although some of these later examples were still fitted with iron ingots, the majority now had spirit lamps mounted on to their bases, their bodies raised above on applied lions' paw supports. One of the most extraordinary pieces made at this time was the 'tea machine' (see page 87), a massive stand fitted with no less than three urns of varying capacities, and a slop bowl. Manufactured by Daniel Holy, Wilkinson and Co. around 1800, and over two feet tall, this was designed to hold hot water, coffee and tea, enabling the family and their guests to serve themselves their choice of beverage. Tea urns sell well today, and one could expect to pay at least £700-£1,000

Over two feet (61cm) tall, this splendid 'tea machine' was probably made by Daniel Holy, Wilkinson and Co. of Sheffield, c.1800. Used on formal occasions, the large urn holds no less than six pints of water. All of the urns can be removed from the stand and used separately for more intimate dinners. It is almost identical to an example illustrated in Bradbury's A History of Old Sheffield Plate, *differing only in having ivory instead of ebony taps. Rare, and extremely impressive, it might well cost as much as £6,000-£10,000.*

A good quality 17½in (44.4cm) tea urn c.1820. It is well proportioned and the claw feet and shell ornaments are well defined. £800-£1,200.

for both early and late examples. Tea machines rarely appear on the market, however, and a complete specimen might well retail for £6,000-£10,000.

Eighteenth century fused plate kettles are scarce and the majority of the few survivors are of a simple tapering oval shape, or with circular bodies chased with narrow, elegant flutes. Supported on drawn wire frames, they were supplied with spirit lamps to maintain the heat of their contents. Far more kettles were made in the 19th century, however, these conforming to current tastes by the addition of floridly-stamped mounts and spouts. Kettles seem to have been popular presentation gifts, and many bear dated inscriptions recording specific events such as weddings or anniversaries. These are, of course, particularly useful to the collector, as they enable unmarked pieces to be dated with a fair degree of accuracy. Large and impressive, 19th century kettles certainly make handsome additions to the modern home. As a result, they usually sell for £400-£600. Earlier specimens appeal, perhaps, more to the collector than to the decorator, and as a result they may well be found somewhat more cheaply.

In the mid-18th century, both sugar and cream were often served from small, swing-handled baskets or 'pails', hand-pierced with arabesques and chased with flutes and swags. Fitted with rich blue or ruby glass liners, these small objects are quite charming, attracting much interest today as they are ideal for holding sweets

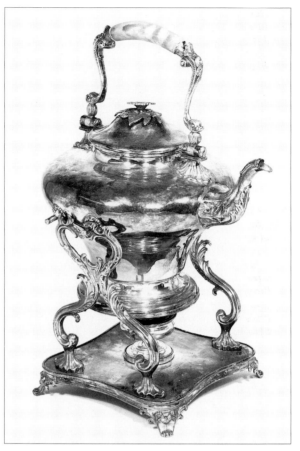

A rare, unmarked late 18th century kettle moulded with horizontal flutes and engraved with a crest which has revealed the copper. The stand, still with its original spirit lamp, is made of fused plate wire drawn through a shaped 'whortle' which has impressed the metal strip with delicate reeding. 14½in (36.8cm) tall, it would now sell for £400-£600.

A good unmarked 22in (55.9cm) kettle on stand, dating from c.1830, with die-stamped scrolling foliate supports. The rim of the stand is applied with drawn fused plate wire to conceal the copper edge. The swing handle is made of bone rather than of ivory, the latter, more expensive, material usually reserved for mounting silver objects. £400-£600.

and nuts. By the 1770s, most were raised on pedestal feet applied with reeding or beading, the design repeated as a strengthening device on the rim. Machine-piercing using a fly punch was now commonplace, the delightful rococo designs gradually giving way to a more elegantly severe but equally attractive neo-classical regularity, with friezes of slats, chevrons, roundels and paterae. Obviously piercing might tend to weaken a piece, so many were stamped with bands of acanthus leaves, adding rigidity to a potentially fragile article. Drawn wire was also extensively used in the manufacture of cream and sugar baskets during this period. Many were made almost exclusively from this newly-invented material, only their pedestal bases manufactured from solid fused plate. A few early cream jugs have been noted, manufactured in the 'helmet' shape so popular in silver in the 1770s. It is possible, too, that small sauce or butter boats were used for serving cream. Nevertheless, survivors are now rare, leading one to assume that the baskets described above were in more common use. Early 'pails' are still available for £150-£200, as are the slightly later pedestal sugar and cream baskets. One could, however, expect to pay £500-£600 for a matching pair, the cream pail an inch or so smaller than its partner.

By about 1780, sugar basins and cream jugs were made en suite with teapots. Oval examples made an appearance first of all, soon to be followed by rounded oblong and then moulded circular specimens. Although it was not necessary for them to have

Another transitional piece from the 1850s, with fused plate body, spout and stand, but with electroplated caryatid handle mounts and fruit finial. Hand-chased with arabesques and engraved with a rococo armorial, it is unmarked, and measures 18in (45.7cm) high. £400-£600.

Three 18th century cream pails or sugar bowls, the earliest, on the left, dating to c.1765. This example is decorated with delightful hand-sawn rococo piercing, and has hand-chased gadroon and rope-twist friezes. The other swing-handled pail, 6in (15.2cm) high, has more regular, machine-pierced decoration executed with a fly-punch. Hand-chased with neo-classical swags of flowers, and with an acanthus leaf chased pedestal foot, this example dates to c.1780. The wirework bowl is unusual, as it is fitted with its original mercury-gilt copper liner. Most pierced or wirework bowls had blown coloured glass liners. This piece dates to c.1780. All are unmarked. Left to right: £200-£250, £150-£200 and £150-£200.

Photo courtesy David Sier, Weston Park Museum, Sheffield

feet, as they did not contain hot liquids, many of the latter were applied with smaller versions of the feet found on contemporary teapots, thus creating a perfect match.

Finely-cut lead crystal sugar basins on wirework frames with round bases became popular in the 1820s. Rather like huge salt cellars, some had an added refinement, a series of eight or twelve wire semi-circles soldered to the rim mount, once used to support a set of teaspoons. Still quite common, George III fused plate sugar bowls and cream jugs might well cost as little as £100-£120. Regency and later specimens are even cheaper, and one could find a good example for £70-£100, although a good cut-glass specimen with a full complement of spoons would retail for at least £250.

A curious relic of the past is the sugar crusher, a small metal disc soldered on to a drawn wire handle. This was used to break up the solid loaf sugar, still on sale well into the 19th century. Fused plate sugar crushers are very cheap. Indeed, I have

recently bought two examples for £1 each, in London's Portobello Road antique market. Perhaps the dealers did not recognise what they had for sale, or, more likely, they thought there would be little interest in such a useless object. While this may be true, it is good to know that one can still buy pieces of 18th century Old Sheffield plate for next to nothing.

Fused plate tea caddies are difficult to find, and are therefore rather expensive. The earliest, manufactured in the 1760s and 1770s, were usually oblong, with bombé sides and hand-chased or die-stamped rococo decoration. Mounted on scroll feet, their detachable lids were applied with delicate scallop shell handles. Made to fit into polished and inlaid wood boxes, they were manufactured in sets of three, two for black and green tea, the third, slightly larger, for sugar. At this period individual caddies were not fitted with locks, as their mahogany or satinwood case could be firmly closed and then locked, thus preventing the servants from consuming the expensive contents. Curiously, this shape became popular again during the reign of George IV, although these later pieces had plain bodies. They are easily recognisable as they invariably have rubbed-in cartouches, a process not discovered, of course, when their earlier counterparts were made.

By the 1780s, this shape had been replaced by a simple oval drum or octagon, occasionally enlivened by some bright-cut or chased swags or ribbons. One could not use a caddy spoon with this type of caddy, as the bowl would not penetrate the narrow neck. Instead, the caddies were fitted with snug pull-off lids, acting as measures for transferring the tea to the teapot. As the century progressed, tea became somewhat cheaper. Consequently, caddies became larger and more ornate. Often made to match tea services, they now stood on display with the rest of the pieces. As a result, they were fitted with tiny but sturdy locks to discourage pilfering. Wooden boxes were still manufactured, but now they usually contained only two caddies, along with a cut-glass basin so that the lady of the house could blend the family's tea exactly to their taste. All caddies are highly sought after by the modern collector, who would have to pay £100-£150 for the smallest, plainest example. Particularly early pieces, or late but attractive caddies, are more

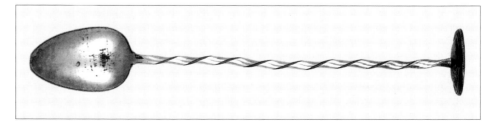

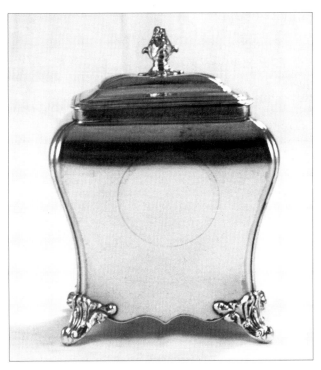

An unmarked octagonal 4in (10.2cm) tea caddy made c.1790, fitted with a tiny lock and with a bone finial. The front is inset with a heavily-plated oval plaque engraved with a vacant shield-shaped cartouche surrounded by delicate floral and foliate engraving. Subjected to many years of use and over-zealous cleaning, this piece is bleeding badly on the cover and on the corner angles. Nevertheless it is sufficiently attractive to be worth £200-£300.

Although this bombé shape is reminiscent of very early tea caddies, this 5in (12.7cm) piece has a rubbed-in silver shield and die-stamped feet and finial, each with seams, features dating it to around 1820. £300-£400.

A set of three 5in (12.7cm) bombé tea caddies in their original satinwood case. They all have the maker's mark of an unidentified maker registered in 1760. The mark was used until 1773 so we can safely date them c.1765. The rococo ornament is die-stamped and the quality very high. Condition of this set is virtually mint and it is very rare indeed. hence £1,500-£2,000.

expensive, retailing for £300-£400, while a cased set of three or two could easily realise £1,500-£2,000, particularly if the wooden box has some fine inlay, and is in good condition.

Trays and Salvers

Salvers and waiters were, judging from their styles, among the first items to be manufactured in Old Sheffield plate. As they were in almost constant use, they were usually made from sturdy metal, plated on only one side at first, the copper backs concealed with tinning. By the 1770s, most were plated on both sides, and were mounted on die-stamped hoof or claw and ball feet. The earliest salvers had stamped shell and scroll borders but this style soon went out of fashion, to be replaced by restrained bead or reed rims stamped in silver. Obviously the makers were not able to engrave their pieces, but the grounds were often delicately hand-

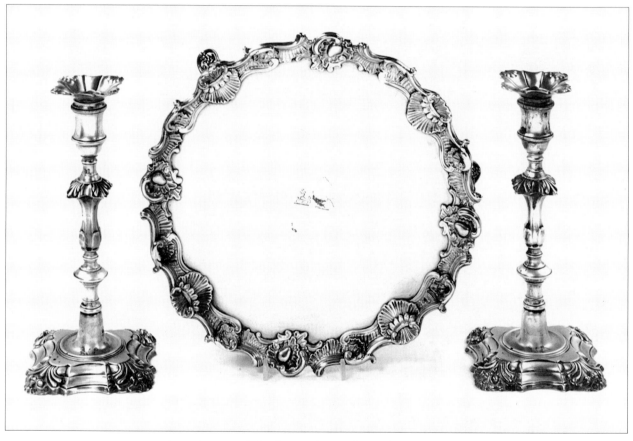

An early unmarked salver made c.1760, applied with a die-stamped rococo border. This style of decoration was soon to become unfashionable, the bold and extravagant asymmetrical curves replaced with the more austere, simple designs of the neo-classical. Made before the introduction of let-in or rubbed-in cartouches, one can see that the engraver has revealed the copper when executing the crests. 11½in (29.2cm) in diameter, it would retail for £200-£400. It is illustrated with a pair of contemporary die-stamped candlesticks, their form closely copying the shape of cast silver sticks dating from the middle of the 18th century. This unmarked pair is 10½in (26.7cm) tall, and could sell for £400-£600.

This elegant, unmarked 22in (55.9cm) tray dates from c.1790. Although, at first glance, one would imagine it is decorated with the bright-cut engraving so popular at this period, in fact both the frieze and the cartouche are lightly hand-chased. Made from copper plated on one side only with silver, the reverse is tinned. Fused plate trays from the 18th century are quite scarce, so one could expect to pay £1,000-£1,500 for this good example.

chased with friezes of rococo scrolling flowers and foliage or, in the third quarter of the 18th century, with regular swags and festoons and with paterae. Most 18th century salvers were circular or oval, the simple outlines facilitating the application of the silver border mounts, but soon the public demanded more extravagant shapes. The manufacturers solved the problem of concealing the copper edges by applying mounts stamped from sheet silver and then filled with solder, burnishing over the edge as described above. Designs for borders became increasingly elaborate as the 19th century progressed, and by 1820 salvers had become florid and somewhat vulgar. The chased grounds also deteriorated, the earlier subtle decoration giving way to a mass of tortured, unhealthy growth, with twisting vines and overblown roses and other flowers.

Trays were made using the same techniques, their handles die-stamped from two halves of fused plate soldered together. Although many handles were strengthened with iron wire as well as with the usual solder, the sheer weight of the trays was often too much for them to bear. As a result, one often finds that handles have snapped, only to be crudely repaired with great blobs of lead solder. Close attention should also be paid to the feet, as these too may have suffered in the same way. Once again, early trays were restrained and delicate, with subtle neo-classical chasing and applied work. Usually oval, and between eighteen to twenty-four inches long, many were applied with friezes of silver, so that they could be bright-cut engraved in accordance with the latest fashion.

A slightly later unmarked tray engraved with the arms of Queen Charlotte, wife of George III. Almost 26in (66cm) in diameter, and made c.1800, this specimen is unusual as the majority of trays were oval or oblong. The handles seem small in proportion to the tray itself, making the piece awkward to carry. Perhaps it was used more for display purposes, resting on a sideboard or buffet. Obviously a royal provenance will greatly enhance the price, and this tray would retail for at least £1,500-£2,000, despite its unattractive shape.

A large and imposing unmarked Regency tray 29in (73.7cm) long, applied with a well defined gadroon, shell and foliate rim turned over at the edge to conceal the copper. The handles are each made from two die-stamped halves strengthened with steel wire and filled with lead solder before assembly. This style of tray has been much reproduced, so one should always carefully check through the points outlined in the section on fakes and reproductions. £1,200-£1,600.

A similarly shaped tray made a decade later, in the 1820s, its appearance marred perhaps by the addition of a broad frieze of chased arabesques. The rubbed-in cartouche with its finely-engraved armorial is clearly visible. This piece is 27in (68.6cm) long, and is also unmarked. £1,200-£1,600.

An attractive 18in (45.7cm) salver made by I. and I. Waterhouse of Sheffield, c.1825. Although the shape is reminiscent of the mid-18th century, the later date of manufacture is betrayed by the chased decoration and by the rubbed-in shield. Examination of the illustration of the mark on this piece (page 217) also shows the over-turned rim, a common feature on pieces of this period. £250-£350.

An unmarked 25in (63.5cm) salver of similar date and design to the previous salver, this example with more elaborate chasing and with die-stamped shells applied to the rim. Large and impressive, it would sell for £700-£1,000. It is illustrated with a set of four Regency candlesticks, two with detachable candelabrum fittings. These sets are always popular, retailing for £1,000-£1,500.

Two 19th century salvers, the larger, 10½in (26.7cm) example unmarked, the smaller example struck with a crossed keys punch used by several different Sheffield companies. Both are worn out through years of over-cleaning, but I illustrate them as they clearly demonstrate the use of rubbed-in cartouches. £30-£50 each, and dear at the price! There are a great number of much better specimens on the market, so these should be left well alone.

A pair of marvellous 14in (35.6cm) salvers by Matthew Boulton, c.1830, with strikingly bold borders, their grounds decorated with extremely fine chasing. Engraved with the arms of Dering, and with unusual upturned rims, these would sell for at least £1,500-£2,000.

The Regency period, however, saw a demand for opulence in both size and decoration. Huge, scalloped oblong trays, some over three feet long, were produced to satisfy this urge. Enormously heavy, one can assume that they were made for show rather than for everyday use, providing a splendid sideboard display. Similar to the salvers described above, they had broad, lavish border mounts and heavily-chased grounds. Because of their size they can carry this extravagant decoration rather more happily than their smaller counterparts. As a result, they are more highly sought after today, examples in pristine condition arousing much interest.

Both salvers and trays were frequent recipients of engraved arms or monograms. Many were inset with silver plates, or had rubbed-in cartouches for this purpose, these processes described above. While contemporary arms enhance the value of an object, one finds, all too often, that later ones have been added. Although these may seem attractive, their presence should reduce the value of a piece to a connoisseur by some twenty per cent. Certainly, they provide excellent grounds for haggling over the asking price, an essential part of the enjoyment of collecting antiques.

Early salvers normally retail for between £200-£400, oval examples usually attracting somewhat higher prices than their circular counterparts. Later specimens are, understandably, more reasonably priced, selling for £100-£200. Trays of all dates are far more expensive, and one could expect to pay well over £1,000 for a good example. These prices only apply to pieces in excellent condition, however. Many fused plate trays and salvers are simply worn out, their grounds, other than the cartouche in the centre, cleaned totally free of silver. Other examples have almost lost their border mounts, again through over-zealous and frequent cleaning, and one can see innumerable grey spots of solder appearing through the remains of the applied rim. Although interesting, as they illustrate the various techniques used in the manufacture of Old Sheffield plate, such pieces should be avoided by the serious collector. It is far better to save up one's money, waiting to buy one

A 10in (25.4cm) salver with die-stamped border and rubbed-in cartouche. This small unmarked piece is rare, as it has only one handle. Originally used by the butler to bring in visitors' calling cards, it was made c.1830. £200-£300.

Photo courtesy David Sier, Weston Park Museum, Sheffield

A late unmarked fused plate tray made in the second quarter of the 19th century. 28in (71.1cm) long, it has a boldly scalloped shape with large and elaborate scrolling foliate handles, echoing the design of the applied rim. £1,000-£1,500. It is illustrated with a salver similar to that illustrated at the top of page 96. This example is not in such good condition however, as copper has started to bleed through the silver skin. £300-£400.

Alcoholic Objects

Our ancestors were enormous consumers of alcohol, so it should come as no great surprise that vast quantities of Old Sheffield plate were manufactured to cater for this demand.

Wine coasters must have been produced in huge numbers, judging from the ease with which they can still be found. Early examples, made in the 1770s, closely resembled contemporary cruets minus handles and feet, their shallow galleries delicately hand-pierced with arabesques. A few years later neo-classical piercing became more fashionable, along with friezes of tiny Gothic arches. By the 1780s, most coasters were pierced using a fly punch, the machine capable of producing some extraordinarily attractive and complex designs when in the hands of a skilled operator. Many coasters of this period could be mistaken for unmarked silver examples, although one can usually detect a seam with a line of silver solder, while engraved arms or initials will inevitably show traces of copper. Gradually the sides became taller, and the simple rims were often scalloped or shaped by the 1790s. Most coasters had small circular bosses inset at the centre of their turned fruitwood bases. These were often made of silver, their hallmarks enabling the collector to date his finds.

The 1790s also saw the introduction of wirework coasters, now often in very poor condition. These, and their pierced contemporaries, must have looked most attractive when fitted with coloured decanters, the bright, rich colours of the glass shining through the gaps to contrast effectively with the silver-covered metal.

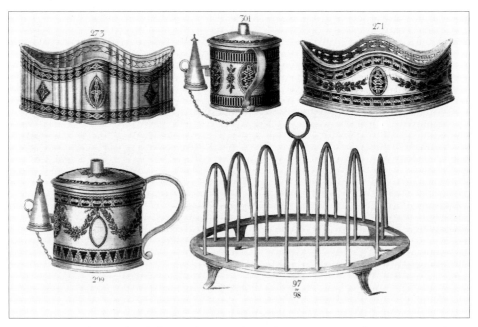

An illustration from a fused plate maker's catalogue dating to c.1790, showing two machine-pierced wine coasters with applied wirework waved rims, one strengthened with vertical fluting. Pairs of coasters are very sought after, usually retailing for £300-£500 if in good condition.

One of a pair of crimson lacquer coasters moulded with horizontal flutes and applied with drawn wire rims and die-stamped lions' mask handles. 5½in (14cm) in diameter, these would sell for £500-£700. Sadly, there are many fakes with electroplated mounts currently on the market, some of them amazingly convincing.

Coloured glass became far less fashionable in the early 19th century, however, following the reintroduction of heavily-cut clear lead crystal. The delicate coasters described above soon made way for much bigger, more ostentatious pieces, designed to show off the sparkling facets of their accompanying decanters. The bombé sides were now rarely decorated with piercing but were left comparatively plain, although some examples were stamped with broad flutes or acanthus leaves. Decoration was now generally concentrated on the everted rims, which were applied with gadrooning, shells and scrolling foliage stamped from sheet silver filled with solder. Modern, electroplated copies of this style have flooded on to the market, but these can be detected quite easily as they do not have the overturned

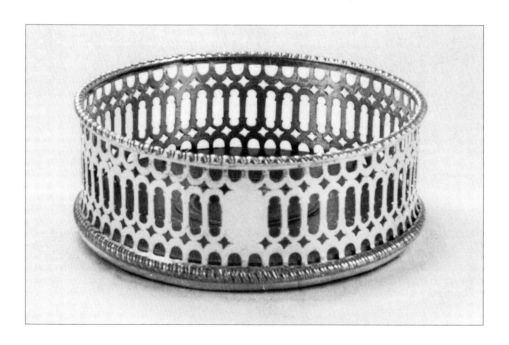

One of a pair of good-looking 5½in (14cm) coasters with piercing of early type, although the borders put it in the 1820s period. £300-£400.

A pair of 1820s 6½in (16.5cm) coasters by Matthew Boulton, decorated with bold spiralling flutes and with die-stamped gadroon, shell and foliate rims. Notice that their turned wooden bases are inset with circular discs or bosses. These are often made of hallmarked silver, enabling the purchaser to date his find with more accuracy than normal. (See Marks, page 217.) £300-£400.

A set of four slightly later unmarked 7in (17.8cm) coasters with more elaborate borders decorated with lavish shells and scrolling foliage. Notice, once again, the circular bosses, this time engraved with monograms, and the seam clearly visible on the example at the front. All fused plate coasters should have a soldered seam, differentiating them from the countless reproductions one can buy today. Sets of four coasters are much sought after, hence £700-£900. The cut-glass liners are not original.

A mid-19th century wine trolley by Walker, Knowles and Co. of Sheffield, c.1840, 15in (38.1cm) long, it is fitted with coasters typical of the period, with fluted, everted rims applied with trailing vines, and with a turned ivory handle. £700-£1,000.

rim which one can feel with a fingernail, and their seam is covered over with silver deposited by electrolysis.

At this time, some manufacturers were making more simple wine coasters with black or bright scarlet lacquered wooden bodies applied with drawn wire reeded rim mounts. While some were left plain, others were moulded with horizontal flutes or were gilt with swags and festoons, while some examples were applied with die-stamped lions' mask handles. These coasters, difficult to date accurately, are now very expensive. As a result, they are being reproduced in large numbers, and the collector should be wary of specimens in mint condition. Sadly, some of the forgers are very shrewd, 'antiquing' their wares with craquelure, a surface finish of fine cracks artificially induced using special varnishes heated in an oven after application. This can be very convincing, particularly as a clever forger will then cover the base of his creations with faded, stained and torn baize, completing the picture to confuse potential buyers.

During the Regency period, wine coasters became increasingly ornate, with very tall sides die-stamped with exuberant flowers and leaves, and with more elaborate rim mounts. Many were still circular, although flaring, fluted examples became popular at this time, these usually somewhat plainer in appearance, but with heavy scroll-moulded rims. Designs became more and more extravagant as the century progressed, and by the 1830s huge coasters with broad, everted rims smothered in trailing vines were fashionable. These are still very popular today.

All wine coasters sell well, as they are both attractive and extremely useful, preventing scratching of polished table tops and also catching any drips which might stain. Early, pierced specimens retail for £300-£500 per pair, 19th century ornate examples probably costing the same. Wirework coasters are slightly cheaper at £250-£350, but good lacquer specimens may well sell for as much £500-£700 per pair. The cheapest are undoubtedly those rather plain examples manufactured in

Above left: *This unmarked early 19th century decanter stand is in remarkably good condition, despite its rather flimsy construction. All of the cut-glass decanters and stoppers are perfect, as is the central bowl, used to hold sugar for sweetening potent spirits. 13in (33cm) tall, it has a plain base on hollow ball feet surmounted by a drawn wirework frame and carrying handle. Notice the applied wire loops, designed to hold the decanter stoppers while the drink is served. £800-£1,200.*

Above: *A later 16in (40.6cm) trefoil decanter stand with elaborate die-stamped shell and foliate handle, a design echoed on the rim mount and on the feet. Manufactured c.1830 and unmarked, the underside of the base is tinned. Once again this piece has all of its original decanters and stoppers in perfect condition, so it would be very much in demand. £700-£1,000.*

This is the type of liquor frame made between about 1790-1810. It is interesting to note that, while the gadroon border round the base is die-stamped in silver, the reeded wire round the decanters has been drawn from plated metal and a little copper is showing. The decanters are blue Bristol, quite beautiful, and typical of the period. Note the letters which appear on the stoppers to avoid confusion and mix-ups. 13in (33cm) high. £700-£1,000.

Two types of fused plate wine labels, the fluted examples dating to c.1790, the more elaborate floral-decorated examples to c.1830. Single specimens can be bought for as little as £10-£15 each unless of a particularly scarce shape, but pairs or sets are far more expensive. The earlier pair illustrated here might cost £70-£100, while the set of four could retail for as much as £200-£300.

the early 19th century. These can still be found, in good condition, for £150-£200. Coasters always sell particularly well in pairs, and there are still some bargains available if one is content to buy single examples, perhaps matching them with similar pieces later on. This happy state of affairs is unlikely to last however, as more and more people are buying odd decanters for both display and use. Each decanter needs a coaster of the correct period so, inevitably, prices for single pieces will start to rise.

Perhaps the ultimate coaster is the wine wagon or trolley, a pair of coasters mounted on leather-bound wheels and with a swivelling handle. These were used on more formal occasions, to pass the wine from guest to guest down a long table. Bradbury states that the trolley was invented in the early 1820s by Sir Edward Thomason of Birmingham, acting upon information received from Lord Rolle, who had dined with King George IV. His Majesty, apparently, 'regretted that his noble guests who sat on either side of him were constrained to rise from their seats to pass the wine' and said to Lord Rolle: "As you have said that you are going to Birmingham tomorrow, you had better call upon Thomason who may invent some plan to obviate this inconvenience". Thomason hit upon the splendid idea of mounting coasters on wheels, sending two silver-gilt trollies to the King, who thoroughly approved the design. This delightful anecdote is, almost certainly, apocryphal, as one may occasionally see a wine trolley which dates, in style, from the late 18th or early 19th century. Bradbury points out, however, that these may

A form of filled-in crescent label not seen in silver. Rather clumsy in appearance, they usually have most of their silver rubbed off. Perhaps they were thinly plated. Circa 1810, £60-£80.

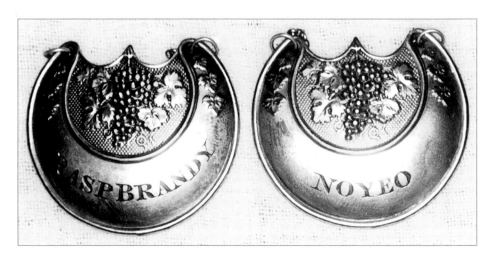

A good pair of late 18th century 8in (20.3cm) wine coolers modelled as buckets, each engraved with the arms of Wallace. Some examples were made with simulated slats of wood bound with metal hoops. It is quite difficult to find pairs of coolers of this simple but pleasing shape in good condition, and this has pushed up their price. Christie's of South Kensington recently sold a pair to the trade for almost £3,000. One can assume that the retail price would be at least £5,000-£8,000.

have been made up from a pair of simple coasters, adapted some years after they were made, to conform with the latest fashion.

The majority of trollies one sees today are certainly post-1820. Fitted with plain, bombé coasters with applied, decorated rims, they are mounted on to large, spoked wheels. Some have elaborate shell-stamped handles, but most are fitted with rib-turned ivory handles, often stained to a beautiful shade of green. Many are also applied with circular mounts designed to hold the decanter stoppers as the wine was poured. All are now very expensive, and one could expect to pay a minimum of £700-£1,000 for a good specimen. Unusual pieces such as the 'jolly boat', a rare form of trolley modelled as a wooden boat, are highly collectable. Usually made in the 1820s, and realistically decorated with simulated planked sides, these were traditionally made for use in naval officers' messes. Today they are rarely seen on the market, so a potential purchaser would have to dig deeply into his pockets, coming up with a retail price of £2,500-£3,000.

Decanter stands were also made in Old Sheffield plate, their shapes closely

A rare and unusual set of three decanter collars of about 1790-1800. The shell and piercing decoration is possibly unique to this type of label. £300-£400.

Campana-shaped coolers were introduced c.1815. Several pairs are shown, giving an idea of the evolution of style from the Regency period through to the mid-19th century. Although they were of one basic shape, this was often masked with varying amounts of applied die-stamped decoration. This 9in (22.9cm) pair is quite simple, with gadroon mounts and vine handles. Unmarked, each has a let-in cartouche engraved with a crest. £3,500-£4,500. They are illustrated with a single Matthew Boulton candelabrum, 25in (63.5cm) tall, its base impressed with his double sunburst punches. Made c.1820, single examples sell for far less than pairs. £1,000-£1,400.

following those of cruets, described above. Early specimens were quite plain, with square or oblong bases applied with drawn wire superstructures. The latter held the decanters, usually four in number, firmly in place, preventing annoying rattling and potential damage, as the heavy piece was passed around the room. In the early 19th century stands designed to hold small spirit decanters were often fitted with central cut-glass sugar bowls. This enabled the host or his butler to mix toddies for his guests, sweetening the potent mixtures to individual tastes. Impressive but eminently practical, complete stands of this period sell for £800-£1,200. By the 1820s more elaborate stands were introduced, with central shell-stamped handles. Most were now of trefoil form, with three slender, bottle-shaped decanters replacing the heavier, square bottles formerly so popular. Mounted on large foliate feet, and with masses of stamped vine decoration, these handsome pieces retail for £700-£1,000, if fitted with original bottles. Empty specimens are much cheaper, of course, as it is very difficult to find decanters of the correct size to fit snugly into the holders.

Although wine labels are quite small, the majority weighing no more than half an ounce, many were manufactured in fused plate, reproducing all of the designs

A slightly later pair of 9½in (24.1cm) coolers enhanced with fluting and with more elaborate gadroon, shell and foliate borders. Made c.1820, this pair was also unmarked.£3,500-£4,500.

Contemporary with the last pair, here we see some unmarked 9½in (24.1cm) coolers chased with broad vertical flutes echoing the gadroon mounts. They are in a rather battered state, hence £2,000-£3,000.

By around 1825 the fluting had become more exaggerated, although the basic campana shape was still much in evidence. This unmarked 9½in (24.1cm) pair has let-in cartouches, the soldered joins concealed by the application of die-stamped silver cartouches filled with lead solder. £3,500-£4,500.

A splendid pair of 10in (25.4cm) Matthew Boulton coolers applied with well-defined scrolling vine decoration and chased with greyhound coursing scenes. Although Boulton produced many similar pairs in the 1820s, the chased scenes are, perhaps, unique, as these were commissioned to celebrate 'Captn. Dunlop's black dog Snowball', which won two coursing events on the 15th and the 19th of February, 1825. One can speculate that the captain ordered these fine pieces, paying for them with his winnings. £6,000-£8,000.

By the 1830s, the campana shape had almost disappeared beneath a mass of chased and applied decoration. Smothered with fluting, grapes and vine leaves, this 10½in (26.7cm) pair was made by T. and J. Creswick of Sheffield, c.1835. The bases are applied with egg and dart friezes, and the handles are more complicated, with stamped satyrs' mask terminals. I find this pair somewhat less attractive than their more simple forebears. This opinion is not shared by many, however, and one could pay as much as £4,000-£6,000 for these coolers.

Sets of four coolers are far more difficult to find than pairs, selling very well indeed. This unmarked 10in (25.4cm) campana-shaped set, made c.1830, is less appealing than some, as they have over-large vertical handles instead of the more usual horizontal handles. They are also quite badly damaged, several of the handles broken off and repaired with great blobs of lead solder. Nevertheless they would retail for £6,000-£8,000.

An 11½in (29.2cm)
Warwick Vase wine cooler
made c.1825, with finely
detailed decoration and
powerful twisted handles.
Unmarked, it may well have
been made by Sir Edward
Thomason, although many
firms soon produced copies
of his originals. £1,000-
£1,500, although a pair
would sell for at least
£4,000-£6,000.

popular in silver, ranging from simple ovals, crescents and oblongs to more elaborate shapes. The first to be produced, in the mid-18th century, failed to copy their silver counterparts with any degree of success. The fashions of this time demanded bright-cut engraving, emulated in Old Sheffield plate with hand-chasing or die-stamping. Sadly, few craftsmen were skilled enough to produce such fine work, and surviving fused plate wine labels now seem somewhat naïve and clumsy, with little of the finesse and elegance of their silver counterparts. Moreover, the majority were made as cheaply as possible, with plating on only one side of the copper. Presumably the makers could argue that no-one would see the back of the label when it was *in situ* around the neck of a coloured glass decanter. Later specimens usually had tinned backs, however, perhaps because there was a risk that the red glow of copper might appear through the clear glass decanters which became fashionable in the 19th century. The names of the various wines and spirits were stamped, avoiding the disclosure of copper on their fronts, and then the letters were filled with black niello to provide an attractive contrast in colour.

Nineteenth century labels were more elaborate in both shape and decoration, with applied stamped border mounts, often incorporating shells and vines. The names of the drinks were now often pierced with a fly punch, although hand-piercing was still used in some of the smaller workshops. Curiously, some of the more unusual names of alcoholic beverages, much sought after by collectors, can be found more easily in fused plate than in silver. T. W. Frost argues, in *The Price Guide to Old Sheffield Plate*, 'It is likely that when some out of the ordinary drink had been acquired, a less expensive label was used because it may only have a limited period of use'.

Single fused plate labels can still be found quite cheaply. Some inexperienced

A pair of very ornate coolers entirely covered with flutes and with attractive waved bases and rims. The naturalistic tendril handles extend into boldly-executed die-stamped swags of vines. 10½in (26.7cm) tall and unmarked, these were made c.1835. £3,500-£4,500.

This pair of unmarked 13½in (34.3cm) coolers was made in the second quarter of the 19th century. Vase-shaped, each is applied with several different friezes of die-stamped decoration, and with elongated handles strengthened with steel wire. This shape is currently less popular than those we have already examined, and one could probably buy them for £2,000-£3,000.

A rare pair of Regency unmarked 9½in (24.1cm) Monteiths, presumably made en suite with some campana-shaped coolers. Applied with bold acanthus leaf friezes, they have detachable wirework rim mounts so that they could be used as punch bowls during the winter months. Single examples are uncommon, and pairs are very scarce, so these would retail for at least £3,500-£4,500.

dealers reject early examples as they have exposed copper backs, dismissing them as poor quality rubbish. As a result, one may be lucky enough to find specimens for a couple of pounds each. Later, more decorative labels are somewhat dearer, although they rarely cost more than £10-£15 a piece. Sets are much more expensive however, and one could expect to pay £150-£250 for three matching labels in good condition. Always check the chains with care, as many will have been broken and repaired over the years. Now they may well be too short for use.

Bottle collars engraved with the names of wines and spirits were also made in fused plate from around 1790-1810. Usually quite simple, their decoration restricted to narrow bands of stamped reeding, they are now very rare, retailing for £40-£60 each, if recognised. A set of three would sell for £400-£500.

Old Sheffield plate wine funnels can still be found quite easily, although the majority of survivors date to the Regency period and later. Rather cumbersome in appearance, with heavy applied die-stamped rim mounts, they sell for £100-£150. Earlier funnels, made during the reign of King George III, are far less sturdy. Manufactured from thinly rolled metal with simple bead or reed mounts, few were strong enough to withstand much use. As a result they are now quite rare, retailing for £250-£300.

Pairs of wine coolers, or 'ice pails' are, justifiably, among the most expensive items of Old Sheffield plate. Handsome and impressive, yet totally practical, they are described by Bradbury as marking 'the culminating point of the platers' craft'. Never cheap, the original wholesale asking price was between fifteen and twenty guineas. Many retailers would have then added a profit margin of about fifty per cent, so it is hardly surprising that purchasers of wine coolers had to be quite wealthy. Many were of aristocratic birth, and one finds that the majority of coolers are engraved with contemporary armorials and crests.

Coolers made before the turn of the 19th century are very rare. Naturalistically modelled in the form of wooden pails or buckets, with moulded and engraved slats and hoops, these pieces are most charming. Their simplicity is much appreciated by the modern collector, who could pay £5,000-£8,000 for a pair in good condition. As the century progressed however, these plain, sturdy coolers went out of fashion. The public demanded more flamboyance for their money, and so part-fluted, squat

A rare pair of unmarked beakers joining together to form a barrel. They are applied with drawn wire strengthening mounts, and each is engraved with a crest which has pierced the silver skin to reveal the copper beneath. Each 4in (10.2cm) beaker has a mercury-gilt interior. Although I have yet to see a complete fused plate set, silver beakers of this form usually contained a picnic or travelling set of knife, fork and spoon along with turned wood or bone condiments. £600-£800.

An attractively simple lidded quart tankard inset with a wooden base and with a wirework thumbpiece. The body and the handle are both seamed, although the lid was made from a hand-raised disc of metal. Notice that the edge of the lid is applied with a silver wire to conceal the copper. Although fused plate tankards are still quite common, this unmarked 9½in (24.1cm) example is in particularly good condition, hence £300-£400.

coolers were introduced, with gadrooned mounts and applied lions' mask and ring drop handles. Somewhat clumsy, these pieces are now less popular, selling for £3,000-£5,000 per pair.

The Regency period saw the arrival of the campana shaped wine cooler, a style based loosely on a form of classical vase. Balanced sturdily on domed circular or square bases, they were now applied with stamped shell and scroll handles, an elaborate decoration repeated in their rim and base mounts. While many examples were left with plain bodies, others were stamped with broad, rising flutes, or were applied with body bands of stamped arabesques. Some particularly fine examples were made by I. and I. Waterhouse, copying the Warwick Vase, a huge Greek vase made of finely carved white marble, owned at this time by the Earl of Warwick. Decorated with a broad frieze of satyrs' masks and vines, and with reeded, elaborately scrolling side handles, the reproduction of this splendid piece proved to be quite a challenge. The task of copying and reducing was eventually given, after some argument, to Sir Edward Thomason. He produced several replicas in bronze by about 1820, which were soon copied in both silver and fused plate. Although the shape was ideal for wine coolers it was also adapted, with less success, for trophy cups, tea urns and soup tureens. Warwick Vase coolers sell very well today, retailing for £4,000-£6,000 per pair. Their plainer contemporaries are almost as popular, selling for £3,500-£5,000.

By the 1830s, the campana shape was largely replaced by the vase shape, usually

A nice beaker, typically plain for its period, 1790-1800. There is a good crest engraved through to the copper. The seam, which is an essential feature, shows well. The value is enhanced by the presence of the maker's mark of Danl. Holy, Wilkinson & Co. on the base. 3¼in (8.3cm). £50-£70.

Three unmarked mugs, each holding about half a pint of liquid. The 5½in (14cm) example on the right is engraved: '1/2 PINT', and was probably used in a public house. Designs for mugs changed little over the years, and they are very difficult to date. I would estimate, however, that these were manufactured, left to right, c.1790, 1770 and 1820. £70-£100 each.
Photo courtesy David Sier, Weston Park Museum, Sheffield

chased with flutes and with applied naturalistic trailing vines. The domed base disappeared in favour of chased foliate and shell feet strengthened with solder, while handles became increasingly elaborate in profile, with stamped grape and vine terminals. These decorative specimens are still very popular, retailing for £3,500-£5,000.

Wine coolers were usually made from copper, plated on one side only, although most had tinned interiors, the white, shiny tin contrasting less strongly with their silver skins. They were invariably fitted with an inner sleeve which slotted tightly into a ring soldered on to the inside of the base. The top of the sleeve was kept in place by a detachable collar, a ring of fused plate which fitted snugly inside the rim of the cooler. This meant that the cooler could be filled with ice before the collar was inserted tightly into place, the sleeve then holding the bottle of wine which was kept away from the melting ice. Perfectly dry, the bottle could be lifted out as necessary, with no risk of marking the table with drips of water. One should never buy a cooler without a sleeve and collar, as it would be almost impossible to find fittings of the correct size. Wine coolers only make high prices when offered in pairs, and single specimens can still be bought comparatively cheaply. Expect to pay no more than a third of the prices quoted for a single cooler.

Monteiths, bowls with wirework rims designed to hold wine glasses, are rare in both silver and fused plate, although examples occasionally appear on the market. Wine glasses were suspended from the rims, their feet held in place by scalloped drawn wire loops, their bowls dangling into crushed ice until the glass was nicely chilled. Early examples were oval, with fixed rims, but many later monteiths had detachable rims, so that the bowl could be used for serving hot punch during the winter. Over the years many of these rims have been damaged or lost, so perfect, complete monteiths now sell very well, retailing for £700-£1,000.

Although claret was usually served from glass decanters, some people preferred to use Old Sheffield plate claret jugs or flagons. Particularly popular in the elegant, neo-classical vase shapes of the late 18th century, many were almost identical to contemporary coffee pots, already described in some detail. They differed only by having short spouts or lips, unlike coffee pots which were usually applied with larger, scrolling spouts issuing forth from the swollen lower part of the body. Fitted

A 6in (15.2cm) two-handled 'loving cup', its shape typical of the 1770s. I would, however, estimate that this was actually made in the mid-19th century. The base is impressed: 'Askew Maker Nottingham' (see page 218), an unusual mark which raises the value to £150-£200, even though the piece is in appalling condition, its body almost entirely cleaned down to the copper.

A sturdy 9½in (24.1cm) brandy saucepan and cover, the latter applied with a silver wire rim mount. Probably made c.1810 but unmarked, this piece would sell well today, at £200-£400.

with delicate polished fruitwood or ivory scroll handles, and with domed, hinged covers with artichoke or pineapple finials, most had subtle decoration restricted to narrow bands of stamped beading, paterae and swags. Later specimens were often stamped with vertical flutes, the effect repeated on the cover and on the wrythen-twist, ovoid finial. It is difficult to say with certainty whether such pieces were designed purely for serving wine. Many of the manufacturers' catalogues illustrate similar pieces as parts of tea services, describing them as hot water jugs. Perhaps they enjoyed a dual purpose, the shrewd buyer making use of his purchase as often as possible. Today, however, they are far more likely to be sold as claret jugs, thus attracting higher prices. Good specimens now retail for at least £300-£400, and I have even seen church flagons, their ecclesiastical inscriptions carefully covered over with applied silver plates, on sale with similar price tags. Sturdy and very plain, the latter rarely sell well, and I was recently able to buy a full Communion set, with flagon, two chalices and a paten, for as little as £120 at a well-attended auction.

In the 18th century, wine was often drunk from gilt-lined goblets. Made to a simple, standard format, they were almost always very plain, their tapering bowls soldered on to rising circular bases stamped with bead or reed rims. Look out for the dentilled seam in the bowl, and for crests or monograms. The latter were invariably engraved through the silver skin, revealing the copper beneath. Goblets are now very popular, retailing for £70-£100 each. Pairs do even better, selling for £200-£300, while a set of half a dozen would cost over £1,000.

Beakers were also fashionable from the 1780s to 1820s. Once again, they were almost always quite plain, their bodies displaying the features described in the previous paragraph. Barrel-shaped examples decorated with simulated hoops and slats enjoyed a brief phase of popularity at the turn of the 19th century, some pairs fitting inside one another to form a compact set for hunting. Similar nests of beakers were made from steer horn, with simple applied fused plate rim mounts and inset clear glass bases. The latter can often be dated, as many were applied with tiny, hall-marked silver, shield-shaped cartouches. Still highly popular, Old Sheffield plate beakers sell well, retailing for similar prices to contemporary goblets. Horn beakers are viewed with less favour by the modern collector, perhaps because they have a tendency to split with changes in temperature. While a complete nest of some half a dozen might reach £300-£400, single specimens usually sell for as little as £20-£40.

Mugs and tankards were made in large quantities in fused plate, many for use in public houses, where they replaced pewter and earthenware to a great extent. Pub tankards were stamped with an imperial measure, and are often in very poor condition, no doubt because they were subjected to a great deal of hard wear over the years. They can be very difficult to date, as many traditional shapes were manufactured throughout the fused plate period, their styles changing little over almost one hundred years. Although mugs were made in both Sheffield and Birmingham, a large number bear the marks of Nottingham makers. Bradbury was able to trace a factory which was still producing fused plate mugs in the late 19th century, well after the general demise of the process, reporting: "although electroplate measures can be supplied at less than half his selling price, still there is a considerable demand for his wares, as they will last three times as long in regular use as those made by his competitors from German silver and electroplated". Thus, one can see that some pieces may be somewhat misleading, their date of manufacture far later than one might suppose. As mentioned above, many mugs may seem much older than they actually are, as they have been battered and over-cleaned during their years of service in public houses.

The shapes of mugs and tankards for home use closely followed those of their silver contemporaries, the earliest examples with plain, tapering bodies and scroll handles. Many had inset wooden bases for greater strength. By the 1770s the swollen, baluster shape had become fashionable, some larger pieces applied with drawn wire body bands, and with domed, hinged lids with stamped scroll or openwork wire thumb-pieces. The early 19th century saw the introduction of the barrel-shaped mug chased with attractive reeded bands, although this design soon fell out of favour, to be replaced once again by the more traditional shapes described above. Today Old Sheffield plate mugs are still quite common, pint-sized examples retailing for £70-£100. Quart-sized specimens are much rarer, however, usually costing at least £250-£300.

Two-handled cups, usually now called 'loving cups', were also produced in large numbers, their simple shapes changing little over a period of some eighty years, so again one may have difficulty in dating a piece with accuracy. Early examples were sometimes chased with fluting and rococo cartouches, some rare pieces bearing the punches of Thomas Law. His punch, a script T.L., was usually stamped several times, presumably in an attempt to copy silver hallmarks. Mounted on domed bases, these pieces sell for £400-£600. Later cups had meaner, smaller bases, and their inverted bell-shaped bodies were left totally plain. Far less popular than their earlier counterparts, they currently retail for £100-£150.

Perhaps the earliest piece of marked Old Sheffield plate is a large brandy pan, stamped with the punch of Joseph Hancock. Formerly in the collection of Frederick Bradbury, and dating to around 1755, this rare object was made from hand-beaten sheet metal plated only on one side, the silver-covered surface on the interior. You can still see this possibly unique specimen in Weston Park Museum, Sheffield, along with many other fine plated items. Later brandy pans were manufactured from copper, plated on both sides. Most were quite plain, with swollen, compressed pear-shaped bodies, but by the turn of the century many were supplied with detachable lids. Even their spouts had tiny, hinged covers, presumably to prevent the loss of any heat to the contents. Fused plate brandy pans are very popular today, as they can be used for serving gravy or cream as well as for their traditional role. As a result they sell well, retailing for £200-£400.

An extremely rare 4½in (11.4cm) fox-head stirrup cup stamped out from two sheets of metal. The line of solder runs the length of the piece through the tip of the nose, as can be seen in the illustration. Although the base has been applied with a fused plate wire, the two ears have not, and so one can quite easily see the copper exposed at their edges. Unmarked but probably made c.1820, the realistically-modelled piece is lined with mercury gilding. £600-£800.
Photo courtesy David Sier, Weston Park Museum, Sheffield

This rare early 6¾in (17.2cm) cup, c.1760, is stamped with Thomas Law's early mark. The decoration follows the pattern of the rococo period in which it was made. £400-£600.

Writing Equipment

Inkstands were very popular items, and the makers of fused plate produced many attractive examples from the 1760s until the mid 19th century. Unfortunately few are still in good condition, the majority displaying a great deal of copper through years of over-cleaning. All too often the original glass bottles will be chipped, and many pieces were fitted with later glass replacements which may well fit rather badly, or seem out of character for the period of the inkstand.

The earliest examples were rather flimsy, so very few have survived. Manufactured before the introduction of silver strengthening edges, their thin metal bases soon buckled and split. Some makers tried to avoid this problem by soldering together two sheets of copper, each plated on one side with silver, but this method was never really successful. Galleried inkstands were introduced in the late 1770s, the majority with delicate piercing created using a fly punch. They were usually fitted with three 'Bristol' blue cut-glass pots, sitting snugly into circular pierced holders which were fastened to the oblong or oval base with long wires passing beneath the inkstand. One pot was for ink, the second was for pounce, powdered gum arabic used to resurface paper which had been scratched with a knife to remove an error, while the third was for sand, which was sprinkled on to fresh writing to dry the ink. Mounted on stamped claw and ball feet made using the same dies employed in the manufacture of cruets and waiters, these charming pieces can still be found for £300-£400.

In the 1790s, boat-shaped inkstands became fashionable. Applied with bead or reed rims, and with wirework superstructures to hold the bottles, these simple pieces were manufactured using existing patterns for snuffers' trays. Converted by the addition of scroll feet, once again 'borrowed' from contemporary waiters, they are still common, retailing for £200-£300. Do beware of snuffers' trays which have been converted at a later date. They are quite easy to detect, as their feet and the

This small unmarked inkstand dates to around 1790. It still retains its original 'Bristol' blue cut-glass inkwell and sander, each sitting snugly inside a machine-pierced holder. Sadly, it is in very poor condition, and you can see that very little of the silvering remains. As a result one could buy this 6½in (16.5cm) piece for as little as £120-£160.

118

The earliest inkstands to be made had proved to be too flimsy. Perhaps this was the reason that this type was made of two sheets of single-side plated metal soldered back to back. The galleries of the cages are of piercing which is typical of the pre-1790 period. This 7in (17.5cm) inkstand is an elegant and very desirable piece worth £350-£500.

tops of their bottles will be made of electroplate rather than of fused plate.

Writing boxes were apparently made in this period too, although I have yet to see a genuine example. Casket-shaped, their hinged, domed lids concealing inkwells and pounce pots, wafer boxes, and pen rests, they are very common in electroplated copper. These later reproductions are frequently offered for sale as 'genuine Old Sheffield Plate', and one could be fooled at a glance by the 'bleeding' of copper showing through the worn silver. In fact, closer examination soon reveals that the entire piece is made of electroplated copper, whereas a fused plate example would have applied silver rim mounts. Although these copies are both attractive and useful, they are hardly worth the £300-£400 usually demanded.

In the 19th century, inkstands became more impressive, their large bases applied with heavy, stamped rococo borders. The inkwells and sanders of this period were often also made of fused plate fitted with glass liners, and many pieces were fitted with central wafer boxes, their lids applied with taper holders for sealing wax. Many of the latter have become detached from their inkstands, as they make charming miniature chamber candlesticks, selling for £100-£150, if complete with detachable nozzle and conical extinguisher. Incomplete inkstands should be avoided, as one can

An attractive unmarked gadrooned inkstand dating from c.1810, moulded with two pen wells and fitted with cut-glass bottles. Fortunately it still retains its original taperstick, designed to hold a stick of sealing wax. 8in (20.3cm) long, this would realise £400-£600. It is illustrated with two pairs of 19th century coasters and a 19th century sauce tureen and cover, similar to examples described earlier.

still find perfect examples quite easily. Highly ornate, they now retail for £400-£600.

A novelty of the early 19th century is the globe inkstand, fitted with two tiny bottles, one for ink, the other, with pierced lid, for sand. Manufactured by Roberts, Cadman and Co., these delightful pieces were designed to copy pedestal library globes, their spherical bodies suspended in a drawn wire cradle, often applied with stamped drapery swags. The covers, the two upper quarters of the sphere, are held in place by a catch released by pressing on the ovoid finial, swivelling on pins and dropping out of sight inside the slightly larger bottom half of the globe. Now very rare, globe inkstands sell for £600-£800, if in perfect condition.

Inkstands dating from the second quarter of the 19th century are often clumsy and ugly. Perched on over-large acanthus leaf and claw feet, and with ostentatious shell handles, they are now fitted once again with cut-glass inkwells. Generally made from thinly-coated copper, they are usually of poor quality, creating a misleading impression of opulence by their sheer size. Good examples sell well, retailing for £400-£600, but the majority are marred by unattractive borders of lead solder, their silver mounts worn away almost completely. Pieces ruined in this way

are, of course, much cheaper than their perfect counterparts, selling for £150-£200.

Old Sheffield plate wax jacks and bougie boxes, cousins of the inkstand tapersticks mentioned above, are now quite rare. Designed to hold long coils of sealing wax, the former were made for desk use, while the latter were portable, their swivelling lids cutting off the oxygen supply to extinguish the flame. Miniature versions of many candlestick patterns were also made, to hold sticks of sealing wax. Today they are all very saleable. Even Bradbury, writing in the early part of this century, says: 'These are all very attractive little ornaments now very much in demand by collectors of Old Sheffield Plate as cabinet specimens and drawing room ornaments'. This enthusiasm is still much in evidence, and prices are remarkably high. Tall tapersticks of candlestick form now retail for £200-£300, while wax jacks may cost £300-£500. Bougie boxes are slightly cheaper, and one can still find simple, pocket examples for £100-£150. Larger pieces decorated with piercing and chasing make more however, selling for £300-£400.

Miscellaneous Pieces

There remain many pieces of fused plate which do not fall happily into any of the above categories. Some are very rare and expensive, while others can be treated quite simply as curios, strange relics of the past, which can still be found quite easily, and which may well be underpriced.

Old Sheffield plate was used extensively, in the late 18th and early 19th centuries, for mounting objects made of other mediums. Lacquer wine coasters have already been mentioned above, and one can also find numerous examples of pottery jugs and mugs with applied reeded mounts, many made by Thomas Law and Co. of Sheffield. Most of these pieces are robust, their coarse pottery bodies applied with hunting scenes or representations of 'Sir Toby Phillpot', but some are surprisingly elegant, with finely-moulded, delicate creamware bodies decorated with classical vignettes in the style of Wedgwood. One can assume that the plate mounts were added primarily as a strengthening device, to protect the rims and spouts from chipping, although some more elaborate examples had fused plate domed, hinged lids with stamped scroll thumbpieces. Bradbury mentions such items, describing them as 'Staffordshire ware', but similar pottery was manufactured elsewhere in Britain, and it seems likely that many of the more primitive items were made of Nottingham salt-glazed earthenware,

An unmarked plate-mounted stoneware ale jug almost 6in (15.2cm) tall, the body applied with rustic scenes, the lid applied with a rim of fused plate drawn wire and with a die-stamped scrolling thumbpiece. These 19th century jugs are underpriced, in my opinion, and one could still buy this piece for £150-£200. It is illustrated with two from a set of four unmarked early 19th century goblets with applied foliate mounts, each with a clearly-visible dentilled seam running vertically up the bowl. Although single goblets can still be found for £70-£100 each, sets are much more expensive, costing £600-£800.

A pair of late 18th century ivory beakers just over 3in (7.6cm) high, each applied with a vacant cartouche, and with a mercury-gilt interior. These rare pieces are impressed with the initials of Thomas Law and Co., of Sheffield. £300-£400 the pair. They are illustrated with a 4in (10.2cm) baluster mug struck with facsimile silver hallmarks. The underside is impressed with a retailer's name: 'Josephus Smith, 141, Moor, Sheffield'. Probably dating to c.1810, this would sell for £70-£100. Photo courtesy David Sier, Weston Park Museum, Sheffield

their mounts created by local metal workers. When buying plate-mounted pottery pay great attention to the condition of the pottery itself. Fractures, and even hairline cracks, reduce the value enormously, as does the loss of any of the applied decoration. Even if the body is good, the mounts themselves can be defective. Manufactured from very thin metal, many are now split where the mount was bent around to fit neatly on to the rim of the body. Lidded jugs and tankards are prone to damage near their hinges. These are often strained and deformed by over-use, ensuring that the lids no longer fit tightly. Although pottery with fused plate mounts is not rare, few pieces are in good enough condition to satisfy the fastidious collector. As a result, one could pay £150-£250 for a fine, perfect lidded quart jug or tankard. Smaller pieces are much cheaper, however, and I have seen beakers priced at only £40-£60. Some examples were obviously made to celebrate special occasions such as births or marriages. Their pottery bodies are impressed with detailed, dated inscriptions, providing a fascinating glimpse of the past. Dated 'documentary' pottery always sells much better than pieces with no definite history, so expect to pay at least double the prices quoted above for any good examples.

One of the largest objects fashioned in fused plate was the plate warmer, a cupboard mounted on scroll legs and fitted with several shelves. Although the front had a hinged door, the back was left open, so that the plates stored inside were heated in front of an open fire. Although brass plate warmers are still quite common, Old Sheffield plate examples are very rare. Dating from the early part of the 19th century, they now retail for £400-£600.

Dish rings, pierced metal bowls designed to support pottery dishes, were once considered to be invariably Irish in manufacture, hence their common name 'potato rings'. In fact, numerous examples were made in Sheffield from fused plate. They were used to protect polished table surfaces from scratching, at the same time raising their contents to create a better display. Moreover, their pierced bodies did not conduct heat so rapidly, thereby avoiding scorching if their contents were hot. First made in the 1770s, early dish rings were hand-pierced with arabesques. Later examples were machine-pierced with more restrained, neo-classical decoration, usually restricted to simple friezes of slats, roundels and foliage. Both types can be

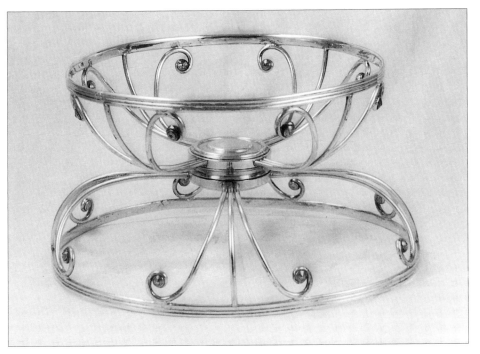

The remarkably effective use that plated wire can be put to is well illustrated here. This whole dish stand is made from wire, with the exception of the central portion. One side would support a circular dish and turned over, the other side would support an oval one. 1790-1800, £200-£300.

found in silver as well as in fused plate, but a variation, made entirely from drawn wire, is very rare in silver. Wire dish rings often had a circular side and an oval side, so that they could accommodate a variety of dishes, although some specimens had two circular holders of different sizes. Examples with two oval holders are also known, but these are extremely uncommon, as are collapsible dish rings, with folding sides. The latter were particularly useful, as they could be adapted to almost any shape of bowl. Wirework dish rings were usually fitted with tiny spirit lamps, now all too often missing. Some were also supplied with cut-glass fruit bowls, so that they could be used as table centrepieces. Pierced dish rings are quite scarce, retailing for £500-£700 if in good condition. Sadly, many have lost some of their pierced work, the edges catching on dusters during cleaning and snapping off. Difficult to repair, such examples should be avoided. Wirework dish rings are cheaper than their more attractive pierced counterparts, selling for £200-£300.

Dish crosses were also used to support hot dishes, their circular centres again fitted

A dish cross, interesting and rare in Old Sheffield plate. This one bears the early mark of Ashforth, Ellis & Co., c.1770. In the centre is a spirit heater. The legs slide along the folding arms, making it a very adaptable dish support. £600-£800.

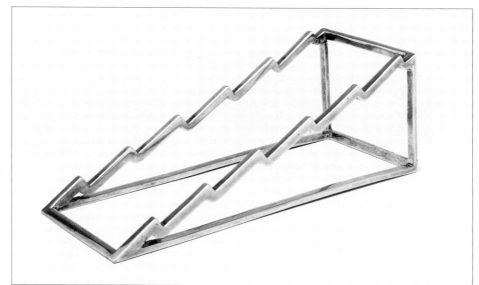

with spirit lamps to maintain the heat of the food. Manufactured from the 1760s until the late 18th century, they were very adaptable, the 'arms' pivoting to hold both circular and oval dishes. Moreover, the actual supporting pads were movable, sliding up and down the arms so that any size of dish could be accommodated. Mounted on shell-shaped feet stamped from two pieces of fused plate and then joined with solder, these attractive pieces sell very well today, retailing for £500-£700.

Dish wedges, used to tilt platters so that all the gravy or sauce could be served, were made in many materials. Bone, ivory and earthenware examples are not rare, and I have even seen a complete set of a dozen small bone wedges, presumably

Two great rarities, a 9½in (24.1cm) fused plate chamber pot and a 10½in (26.7cm) bordaloue. The function of the first is quite obvious, even with today's more sophisticated plumbing, but I should, perhaps, explain the latter. Bordaloues were chamber pots designed for daytime or evening use by ladies, who wore too many underclothes to get undressed when nature called. The Georgians were less embarrassed by bodily functions, and would simply squat down and pass water, whether at the theatre or at dinner with friends. Both pieces are unmarked, and date to the last quarter of the 18th century. £400-£600 each. Notice that the chamber pot is plated on the outside only, although the bordaloue was manufactured from copper plated on both sides. Photo courtesy David Sier, Weston Park Museum, Sheffield.

used to raise up soup plates. Old Sheffield plate wedges are much scarcer, however. Made of drawn wire, they are usually stepped, so that one could vary the angle of tilt. Three to four inches long, they might well cost £100-£150, if recognised by the dealer. One is equally likely to find them for a few pounds in junk shops and flea markets, their age and former use totally unknown and therefore un-valued.

Fused plate cucumber slicers are fascinating gadgets, now extremely rare. They consist of a hollow cylinder mounted on to a circular base. A cucumber is placed inside the cylinder and held in place by a group of sharp spikes mounted on to a metal disc. This moves forward as the fruitwood handle is turned, gradually forcing the cucumber out of the cylinder. The handle is also fitted with a steel blade, usually scimiter-shaped, which cuts the fruit into thin slices as it is ejected. These totally practical objects are not mentioned in Bradbury's exhaustive book, perhaps because he simply did not come across an example during his many years of dealing in and collecting Old Sheffield plate. It is very unlikely that one could find a cucumber slicer on the market, and it would therefore be impossible to predict an accurate retail price. Anyone who wishes to see this curiosity should go to Sheffield City Museum, which has an example in its fine collection of fused plate.

Another great rarity is the honey hive, a skep-shaped honeypot realistically-stamped with a simulated basket-weave effect and mounted on a stand with curved scroll legs. Examples in silver are known, many by the celebrated silversmith Paul Storr, his pieces often applied with tiny, well-modelled honey-bees and with a bee finial. Such charming refinements were impossible to reproduce in Old Sheffield plate, so the manufacturers of the latter contented themselves with delicate loop handles made from drawn wire. Standing only six inches tall, and yet modelled with great realism, fused plate honey hives are absolutely delightful. This, combined with their scarcity, ensures very large prices, and one could expect to pay £600-£800 for an example in good condition.

Telescopic toasting forks were, apparently, introduced by Sir Edward Thomason, who wrote in his memoirs 'In 1809 I invented the sliding toasting fork, some with one, two or three slides, within a handsome japanned handle common now in all the shops'. He went on to complain '…but as I did not protect this invention by patent, thousands were made and sold by other manufacturers'. Some simply had sliding stems, so that one could make toast without getting too close to the open fire, but others were more sophisticated, with hinged shields which held the bread

Possibly unique, this wonderful fused plate table can now be seen in Sheffield Museum. Almost 4ft (121.9cm) long, it is a tour de force of the platers' skill, representing many hours of work, and employing every technique available to them. The chasing on the top is of the best possible quality, while the die-stamped mounts are quite superb. Amazingly, this piece is unmarked, but one can date it by style to c.1825. Needless to say, it is impossible to price, but I would hazard a guess that it could retail for at least £15,000-£20,000.

Photo courtesy David Sier, Weston Park Museum, Sheffield

A pierced and engraved 10½in (26.7cm) pipe lighter of c.1785. Its copper lining is missing. This is a very early example of a silver wire edge. Note that the ball and claw feet are riveted to the body, as is the handle. £500-£700.

firmly on to the spikes, thus preventing the risk of it falling off into the flames. Thomason wrote 'The above were made in silver, gilt, plated and brass, and large quantities were sold…'. Despite this, examples in all mediums are now scarce. Although I have seen several silver telescopic toasting forks, I have yet to see a fused plate specimen. One can speculate that they were simply thrown away when gas and electric toasters were introduced, their silver cousins surviving only because of the intrinsic value of their metal content. Despite their great rarity, however, I would not expect to pay more than £150-£200 for a fused plate toasting fork, relying on the fact that many collectors prefer larger, more showy pieces.

The Demise of Old Sheffield Plate

From about 1830, the copper base of fused plate was gradually phased out, to be replaced by German silver or Argentine, an alloy of copper, nickel and zinc. Apparently introduced to Sheffield by a Berliner, Herr Guitike, this alloy was harder and more durable than copper. An even greater advantage lay in its colour, a whitish grey. At a glance this resembled the silver skin, and any bare patches caused by over-zealous cleaning were far less noticeable than those on fuse plated copper. Manufacturers were now able to use much less silver on their wares, thus saving a great deal of money. Unfortunately, the white alloy was liable to oxidise and decompose, particularly if exposed to water. As a result, many makers continued to manufacture items of fuse plated copper, introducing the new material only where contact with water seemed unlikely.

Samuel Roberts of Sheffield was one of the first makers to use German silver. Others soon followed suit, and by the mid-1840s the majority of articles were made entirely from German silver, or from a combination of fuse plated copper and German silver, the former often employed for the bodies of pieces while the latter was used for applied details, such as handles and feet.

Electroplating, a new process for covering base metal with silver and gold, was introduced commercially in the 1840s, although the jury at The Great Exhibition of 1851 selected only Old Sheffield plate for a prize medal, presenting the award to the firm of T., J. and N. Creswick for pieces 'plated by the old style of uniting metals by heat, with edgings and mountings of silver'. The jury especially praised their Louis XIV and Louis XV style candelabra, and commended the workmanship of the company as 'carefully executed, and perfectly adapted for long use'. The new technique of electroplating was mentioned by the jury, who rather hesitantly praised 'the artistic application of this discovery, to which alone they are inclined to think it adapted'. Elkington's spectacular designs were admired, but the jury were nervous of any major innovations within such a well-established industry. They obviously were not convinced that the process could produce a durable plated finish, suggesting that it might be useful for ornamental pieces, while refusing to comment on its employment 'for objects of domestic use'.

Despite these misgivings, electroplate soon swept the board. Much cheaper to produce than fused plate, for reasons discussed in the next chapter, it replaced the technique of heat fusion within a few years. Some manufacturers were able to adapt to the new process, producing transitional objects with fused plate bodies and electroplated knobs, handles and feet. These more adventurous makers swallowed their pride and invested money in the new technique, adapting their factories and retraining their workforce to cope with the newly-invented process until they were soon able to compete with Elkington and Co. in the production of articles made entirely from electroplate. Others were unable or unwilling to change, however, stubbornly sticking to the established methods of plating. Inevitably they suffered from both price undercutting, and from the introduction of new designs, impossible to reproduce in fused plate. Sadly, many companies were pushed out of business into bankruptcy, their premises and staff taken over by their more aggressive and up to date competitors.

The Care of Old Sheffield Plate

Throughout this chapter, I have insisted upon good condition as an essential pre-requisite to purchase, stressing that one should buy the very best articles that one can afford. It is far better to be patient, buying one excellent item rather than half a dozen second or third-rate pieces. Damaged, repaired or worn fused plate should always be left for someone else, unless the piece is particularly rare, filling a gap in an otherwise complete collection.

Much Old Sheffield plate is marred, to a greater or lesser extent, by 'bleeding'. This term refers to the red glow of copper which may appear through the thin silver skin of pieces which have been over-cleaned or simply over-used, the latter causing wear in certain areas constantly touched by the owners over a number of years. Thus, tankard handles are often more badly worn than their bodies, and the interior bases of snuff boxes frequently bear two rubbed marks, caused by the owner's fingers as he took his pinches of snuff. A small amount of bleeding is inevitable on early items engraved with arms or initials, before the invention of inset or rubbed-in cartouches, as explained above. Many collectors like to see some bleeding, preferring the warm hues of copper to the cold whiteness of silver. Nevertheless, it should be avoided where possible, and one should certainly never buy pieces where almost all the silver is worn away, leaving behind only the applied rim mounts and the rubbed-in cartouche. Bleeding is often a problem with later pieces, made as cheaply as possible, in the second quarter of the 19th century. Many manufacturers used increasingly small amounts of silver on their wares during this period, economising to produce pieces which appeared to be of excellent quality, but which soon wore out.

Years of over-cleaning and use may also have damaged the applied, stamped silver rim mounts, handles and feet. Salvers seem particularly prone to this, and I have seen many examples where the silver has completely worn away, leaving ugly solder mounts exposed on the surface. Some are less badly damaged, and one should always examine mounts with great care, checking for spots of solder appearing through the die-stamped silver. These can invariably be seen on the highest parts of the decoration, as these areas suffered more from rubbing during cleaning. Once again, these pieces should be avoided where possible.

Regrettably, a great deal of worn Old Sheffield plate has been disguised with later electroplating, this process effectively concealing both exposed copper and solder, as well as any repairs. Unfortunately it also covers all of the features which make fused plate so interesting, as they show us the various techniques used in manufacture. Thus, over-turned rims, dentilled joins, and rubbed-in shields are all covered by a uniform layer of silver. Although an electroplated piece of fused plate may appear, at first glance, to be in excellent condition, its appeal to the more knowledgeable collector has been lost for ever. One should never have pieces re-plated, however poor they may be. Unfortunately many of the public do not realise the folly of this action, and I have seen many fine pieces which have been completely ruined. Indeed, some of our customers proudly announce "They were a bit shabby so I had them 'dipped' before I showed them to Christie's". I then have to explain that any interest to collectors has been lost, and that the value is subsequently greatly reduced. It seems a pity that some plating firms ruin Old Sheffield plate in this way, either through ignorance or greed, instead of advising their potential customers not to tamper with worn pieces. Fortunately, fused plate which has been re-plated can usually be recognised. Electroplating deposits pure silver rather than sterling standard silver, so the overall effect is too stark and white.

Perhaps the best advice one can give, is to look very carefully at pieces which are in mint condition. After all, fused plate objects were made to be used, and it is therefore extremely unlikely that pieces will have survived which are perfect in every detail. Inevitably, there should be some wear, even if it can be seen only under the feet, scratched from contact with the tops of tables or sideboards.

A new chemical product on the market covers selected areas of wear with silver plating. Ideal for concealing small bare patches, it is much more difficult to spot. The collector may well buy a piece which seems in good condition but, after a few attempts at cleaning, areas of copper or repairs are revealed, the newly-applied silver coating simply wiping away. This type of concealment is more difficult to see, and one can only rely on the integrity of the trade, who should inform the prospective purchaser if a piece has been treated using this new process. Antique shops are, perhaps, safer hunting grounds, as one can always take an item back after a few weeks, if it fails to live up to expectations in this way. Many antique fairs and markets are rather changeable, with a high turnover of both goods and dealers, so one is far less likely to be able to return faulty merchandise. Moreover, many sellers might well be reluctant to refund the purchase price, arguing *caveat emptor*. One can only use an indefinable second sense when buying, judging both the goods themselves, and the person who is selling them.

Assuming you have found and bought a piece which is still basically sound, you will then need to clean it, removing many years' accumulation of grease, dirt, tarnish and old polish. The first step is to wash the item in hot, soapy water. This removes surface dirt and also loosens any packed deposits. Try not to soak wooden or ivory mounts, as these can soon split if exposed to water. Although smooth, flat surfaces may well be quite bright after washing, the decorative mounts are usually in a very poor state, all their details masked with black deposits. Pierced or wirework items are particularly difficult to clean, and one needs to rub them vigorously with a small, stiff brush, using a paste of ammonia and whiting. Take care to do this outside, weather permitting, or at least in a well-ventilated room, as the ammonia fumes are very unpleasant. Using a circular brushing motion, ensure that the bristles penetrate all the small crevices and depressions to loosen the dirt. Reeded mounts are best cleaned by stroking firmly along the reeding, but beading responds best to the circular action mentioned above.

Although ammonia and whiting will clean most pieces, some are simply too filthy. These can be treated with silver dip, a clear, powerful liquid which will penetrate the most stubborn deposit of grime. You must be careful however, as this may well mark the surface if left on for too long. It must always be washed off as soon as possible, so it is better to attack small areas with dip, concentrating on individual patches of dirt. The piece should then be rinsed with clean water and dried, before another place is treated.

Once you have cleaned a piece to your satisfaction, it must then be polished. Avoid cream polishes which feel gritty, as the tiny, hard particles they contain will scratch the surface, leaving behind a network of fine marks. Some proprietory brands of cleaners are better than others, many with the advantage that they impart a long-lasting shine. Silver-cleaning foams are less harmful than some creams, but unfortunately their effect is more limited. As a result, your pieces will need polishing more often, removing a microscopic layer of the thin silver coating to the eventual detriment of your collection. Creams and foams can be applied with clean, soft cloths, although detailed decoration is best tackled with special silver-cleaning brushes with soft bristles. Another brush can then be used to polish these areas, removing any white deposits of dry cream at the same time.

One should really try to clean fused plate as little as possible, as each time you get closer to the copper beneath. It is better to simply wash items in soapy water, rinsing them afterwards in clean water, before drying with a soft cloth. 'Long term silver cloths' are particularly useful at this stage, as they are impregnated with a chemical designed to maintain the lustre. Indeed, these cloths are very useful for regular cleaning, each piece needing only a few seconds of gentle rubbing. It is far better to clean plate little and often, rather than to leave it until a more thorough overhaul is necessary.

Pieces which are exposed tarnish more quickly, their silver surfaces reacting with sulphur in the atmosphere to produce silver sulphide. Although our cities are far cleaner than in the past, there is still a great deal of sulphur present in the air we breathe, much of it produced by open fires and even central heating. Cigarette smoke also causes tarnish, as well as leaving behind an unsightly deposit of yellow nicotine. Items kept behind glass will tarnish more slowly, and it is better to display a collection in this way if possible, using a china cabinet or glass-fronted shelves. Obviously, this would not be appropriate for many of the larger, more spectacular, specimens of Old Sheffield plate, which need to be displayed on a large table or sideboard. Many choose to have such items lacquered, but I feel this spoils the appearance, masking both colour and brilliance. Moreover, the lacquer surface is very fragile. A small knock may well chip the air-tight finish, allowing tarnish to creep underneath. This soon spreads, causing an unpleasant, crackled effect which is difficult to remove.

Pieces which are not on display can be stored in dry conditions, wrapped in sulphur-free tissue paper which can be bought from jewellers and milliners. Never wrap your collection in old newspaper, as this material actually contains sulphur, and will promote the rapid formation of tarnish. Moreover, newsprint often contains acid, and I have seen pieces which have been wrapped in newspaper and then stored away in bank vaults for many years. They are inevitably ruined, the newsprint etching into the surface to disfigure the silver. Marks caused in this way can be polished away professionally using a buffing-machine, but there is a great risk that the piece itself will be damaged by such drastic means, the machine removing the thin silver skin to expose the copper beneath.

It is extremely difficult to repair damaged Old Sheffield plate successfully. Most restorers of antique silver will simply refuse to tackle fused plate, although small parts such as feet, finials, or thumbpieces can be remade by casting. If you do wish to have a cherished piece repaired in this way, then the missing elements must be cast in sterling silver. They will then match the colour of the sterling skin on the rest of the item, and will also tarnish at the same rate. Needless to say, such a repair would be extremely expensive, the cost probably outweighing the value of the object itself. Consequently, it should only be considered if the item is of great sentimental rather than monetary value.

Many specimens have been repaired, in the past, with soft lead solder, this amalgam melting at a much lower temperature than silver solder. Its use ensured that splits could be repaired with little risk of causing further damage by melting the original silver solder with an overheated soldering iron. Most repairers made little attempt to hide their work. After all, they were simply restoring pieces so that they could be used once more on a day to day basis, rather than working on objects which were considered, at the time, as valuable collectors' items. As a result, many pieces of fused plate are marred with great floods and blobs of ugly lead solder. Teapots and candlesticks are particularly prone to such disfigurement. They should be left well alone, as only electroplating can disguise such obvious faults.

Fakes and Reproductions

There are a great number of pieces of reproduction Old Sheffield plate on the market, although many are not fakes, in the strictest sense of the word. It would, of course, be perfectly possible to reproduce the manufacturing techniques of fused plate, described in detail above. Bradbury, writing in 1912, mentions pieces: 'made in Sheffield entirely in the old way, from fused plate with silver shields and mounts, and with silver threaded edges'. He goes on to point out the disadvantage of this manufacture, stating 'The expense is so great in making that they have to be sold at about the same price as antique articles, and naturally they lack that mellowness of appearance, given by age, which is the best test of antiquity'. While the last test is difficult to describe, his first point is still valid. Indeed, the cost of specialised labour and knowledge has risen enormously since the beginning of the 20th century, and one can safely say that it would now be impossible to produce totally convincing fakes of Old Sheffield plate on a financially viable scale.

Straightforward reproductions made from electroplate are quite easy to detect in a number of ways, despite the fact that makers have studied the designs of old plate with care to produce pieces which may, at a glance, seem quite convincing. Some were, and indeed still are, made of electroplated nickel while others employed copper as the base material, sometimes lending a spuriously convincing air, as the electroplate may be worn, revealing the glow of copper beneath. Newly electroplated objects are cold in appearance, the pure silver used in the process over-bright and somewhat forbidding. The sterling silver used to make fused plate is more mellow, with a lovely tinge of colour produced by the copper used in the silver alloy. Unfortunately, this test is very arbitrary. One would need to have two pieces side by side, one electroplated, the other plated by fusion, before a substantial difference in colour could be seen. Similarly, Bradbury says that one should avoid 'ill-shapen specimens' or 'any articles of rough workmanship', claiming that they are always reproductions. These are dangerous simplifications, no doubt caused by the great love and enthusiasm which Bradbury felt for fused plate. I have seen lots of perfectly genuine pieces of Old Sheffield plate which are badly designed and remarkably ugly, and many very early objects were often crudely made, the manufacturers lacking sophistication of technique in the 1750s and 1760s.

The means of differentiating between Old Sheffield plate and electroplate described in the above paragraph are not very useful for the inexperienced collector, who needs less arbitrary tests. Fortunately these are available, and one merely has to learn the various techniques used in the manufacture of fused plate, described at length above, applying this knowledge to look out for the tell-tale signs. For example, one will be unable to detect let-in shields or dentilled seams on reproduction pieces, as the entire surface of the object has been electroplated after construction, the silver skin concealing such details. Bradbury mentions the fact that, after about 1790, the majority of genuine large and medium-sized fused plate objects had silver shields for the engraving of crests. If you find a piece without this feature, then it should be treated with caution. There is every chance that it is a reproduction or, at the very least, a period object which has been later electroplated. Similarly, as electroplate is covered with silver after assembly, any solder used in the process will also be covered with silver. Examine the undersides of objects with care, and if any solder bears traces of plating, then the piece cannot be a specimen of Old Sheffield plate in original condition.

Applied mounts, whether simple beading or reeding, or more florid shells and

A group of objects copying Old Sheffield plate styles. The two tea caddies and the candlesticks have applied cast copper mounts, instead of die-stamped silver mounts, while the bowl has a cast copper gadroon rim and cast mask feet. The candlestick stems also lack the seams one would expect to see. Made to deceive, the 11in (27.9cm) candlesticks are engraved 'Sheffield Plate on Copper'. The other pieces are copies rather than forgeries, although a proud owner of the caddy on the left stuck on a paper label inscribed 'Rare and early Old Sheffield Plate, 1765'. £20-£100.

scrolling foliage, were always made of silver, sometimes, but not always, filled with lead solder. Die-stamped with new, sharp steel dies, they were invariably filled with clear-cut detail. Although some reproductions are made using the old dies, the dies are now worn with use, creating a blurred effect. Attempts have been made to cut new dies, but these are of poor quality, producing rough stamps which cannot compare with those of the past. Moreover, most reproduction pieces have mounts stamped in copper and then electroplated after being soldered into position. Wear of the plating on these mounts will reveal copper, proving that the piece is made of electroplate.

The makers of Old Sheffield plate never used casting to manufacture any of the components of their wares. Instead, solid features such as feet, handles and finials were made from two or more pieces of die-stamped sheet metal filled with lead solder. As a result, one can usually detect a soldered seam dividing these components. Reproductions, on the other hand, have cast pieces, which are soldered into place before the object is electroplated. Close examination with a powerful magnifying glass will reveal many tiny pits caused by air bubbles, and the surface will be textured with a granular appearance caused by the sand used in the casting moulds. Many reproductions also have cast gadroon mounts, these too marred with air bubbles and a rough finish.

Finally, one should bear in mind that many pieces of fused plate were made from copper coated on only one side with silver. This side was exposed to view, while the part which could not be seen was left bare or, more often, was covered with tin. In contrast, electroplating covers the entire object, and one finds that the undersides of meat dish covers and the insides of teapots have an equally thick deposit of silver, although these areas cannot be seen, and are subjected to far less wear.

Electroplate

Introduction

Electroplating, a relatively new process first carried out on a commercial scale in the mid-19th century, has created a comparatively new collecting craze. As recently as 1986 Joy D. Freeman, a Connecticut dealer in American plate, tried to dispel some myths in an article published in *Silver* magazine, concluding, 'There is nothing inferior about electroplate – in fact it's several rungs on the ladder ahead of heat fusion. It is so good in fact, that the method is virtually the same as it was when developed almost 150 years ago… far from being all machine-made with no intrinsic value, 19th century silver plate had a wealth of hand work on it. This, plus its historic value, gives this medium as much intrinsic value as any of the great decorative accessories of the era'.

Similarly, Sam Wagstaff, owner of an important collection sold by Christie's in New York in 1989, felt obliged to write an explanatory introduction when he exhibited his splendid pieces at the New York Historical Society. He wrote 'The aesthetic of (electro) plate of the great period in the United States (probably 1875-1895) passed quickly like a comet and has left almost total ignorance and total disfavour. All the better for those few crazies like myself who enjoy its perversity and are trying to assemble nuggets of it…'.

Happily, both of these experts were, to a large extent, preaching to the already converted. Certainly, *Silver* magazine now includes a great number of fascinating

A rare wirework toast rack designed by Dr. Christopher Dresser and made by James Dixon and Sons, of Sheffield. 6½in (16.5cm) high, this very collectable piece with impressed signature sold for no less than £13,000 plus 10% premium, when offered at auction by Christie's of St. James' in September, 1988. It could retail for as much as £18,000-£22,000. Some Dresser-designed pieces are now immensely valuable, the modern collector appreciating their avant-garde style, which was many years before their time.

A simple globular cream jug and sugar basin, again made by James Dixon and Sons, each piece impressed with the facsimile signature of Dr. Dresser, and with a diamond patent registration mark, used between 1842 and 1883. The mark on these objects indicates that their design was patented in 1880. (See page 218) £1,500-£2,000.

A wonderful 30in (76.2cm) palm tree centrepiece applied with Bedouins and their camel. Notice that it still has the original mirror plateau, although the glass bowls are now missing. This piece, representing the height of Victorian naturalism, would be impossible to make in fused plate. It is typical of the kind of ornate object which found such enormous favour in the mid-19th century, helping the Elkingtons to prosper at the expense of their more traditional rivals. The underside is applied with a plate engraved 'Published by Elkington and Co., May 1860'. £1,200-£1,500, despite the lack of bowls, as the subject is very appealing to the Middle Eastern buyer.

articles on plate, while the results of the Wagstaff sale were quite staggering. Prices for decorative pieces of plate soared above pre-auction estimates, as collectors strove to buy charming or impressive examples.

This tremendous interest in electroplate is not confined to America. European buyers are now prepared to part with large sums of money for unusual or decorative objects. It is sometimes difficult for the salerooms to keep up with these prices, as pairs of entrée dishes or teasets still estimated at around £100 now often sell for £200 plus. Cartons of miscellaneous pieces also do very well, as both private and trade buyers sort through the oddments, calculating the value of each item along with the cost of re-plating or repair. The demand for electroplate is so great that many dealers sell nothing else, providing a steady stream of fresh objects to delight their customers.

No longer viewed as a cheap substitute for silver or Old Sheffield plate, electroplate is now collected in its own right, many wealthy buyers eschewing traditional objects to concentrate on well-designed pieces of more recent manufacture. Demand is particularly strong for Arts and Crafts items, especially those designed in the late 19th century by Dr. Christopher Dresser. Pieces which bear his facsimile signature can sell at auction for several thousands of pounds, far outstripping their silver counterparts of the previous century. Novelty pieces and naturalistic creations are also immensely popular, and the demand for good electroplate is still growing steadily as more and more collectors are seduced by its charms.

The Process of Manufacture

The great savings in cost in the manufacture of electroplate resulted primarily from the fact that objects were assembled before plating. Seams and soldered joints did not need to be disguised, as the plating process deposited an even layer of silver over the entire piece, however complicated it might be, covering up all the signs of construction which caused so many problems for the makers of fused plate. Moreover, a great number of the components could now be cast in solid metal, doing away with the time-consuming and therefore expensive stamping out of mounts, handles and feet, which all had to be filled with lead solder before they could be applied to each piece.

Many base metals could be used to fashion the objects and, in practice, two or more different materials were often used for the various components. Thus, the properties of each metal were fully exploited to their best advantage. Malleable materials like brass were spun or hammered into shape to form the bodies, while harder alloys were cast to form decorative details. The best metals were felt to be copper, brass and German silver or nickel silver, an alloy of copper, nickel and zinc. The latter was particularly popular, as it proved to be hard and durable. Moreover, its colour, a very pale yellow, was far less obvious than copper if the plating wore off after several years of cleaning. Britannia metal, an alloy made primarily of tin with small proportions of antimony and copper, was also used a great deal, often for cheaper wares. This alloy was rather soft and malleable, which meant that objects were all too easily dented. Nevertheless, it was often used for holloware such as tea and coffee pots, particularly in the late 19th century as, once again, its silvery grey colour was not too noticeable if the piece was over-cleaned. German or nickel silver was still preferred, however, for cutlery and for other pieces which had to be able to withstand heavy use.

Once the piece was created, it was boiled in a caustic alkaline lye. This removed any traces of grease left by the workers' hands, as the smallest trace of grease would prevent the deposition of the silver. The lye was then washed off, and the piece was thoroughly dried. It was then dipped into dilute nitric acid which removed any oxides which might have formed on the surface, washed in clean water, and then suspended in a solution of silver dissolved in potassium cyanide and water. Electricity generated by batteries was passed through the solution, the power causing the silver to leave the solution by electrolysis, forming an even layer over the entire surface of the suspended object. The batteries had to be regulated with great care, and there were many failures in the early days of electroplating. If they were too weak, then a very soft layer of silver was created, while if they were too powerful, the silver was deposited in an unworkable powdery form. Once the correct strength of electricity was achieved, however, 'the silver will be equal in hardness to rolled or hammered silver'. Usually the solution was heated, as it was found that the hotter the liquid, the less battery power was required for successful plating.

The piece had to be left in the solution for only a few seconds at first, then it was taken out and thoroughly scratched with a brush made from fine brass wire. This ensured that subsequent layers of electro-deposited silver could form a firm bond with the surface, adhering closely to the thousands of tiny scratches. The piece was then submerged once again into the silver solution and left for several hours, until the requisite thickness of plating was deposited. Obviously, the quality of goods varied considerably, depending on the length of time that they were left in the fluid. Many firms prided themselves on their 'double' and 'triple' plated wares, suggesting that any extra cost was far outweighed by their much longer life. Others cleverly plated certain components of their wares before assembling the pieces, afterwards re-plating the whole object once again. This method, known as 'sectional plating', was used in areas where one would expect the most wear to take place. Thus, teapot handles and feet were sectionally plated before being soldered to the body, while spoons were often half-submerged into the silver solution so that the backs of their bowls received an extra coating of silver. When the whole piece was subsequently plated once more, the varying thicknesses of the silver deposit ensured a longer life.

Some firms even went to the trouble of soldering small inlays of silver on to the handles and on to the backs of the bowls and prongs of spoons and forks, before each piece was shaped and plated. This was to prevent rapid wear caused by friction, as the pieces were placed on the dining table. The process was patented in 1887 by William A. Warner of Syracuse, New York, a small producer of cutlery. He was approached by partners Holmes and Edwards of Bridgeport, Connecticut, who signed him on to work for them. They streamlined the process, introducing mass-production techniques and, by 1892, had won a gold medal at The World's Fair Columbian Exposition for 'the greatest improvement in plated flatware in a hundred years'.

Once the piece had a sufficient coating of silver, it was removed from the solution. Inevitably it had 'the matted appearance of dead silver', with an unpleasant, chalk-white finish. This was removed by scratching with a fine wire brush dipped in old ale or beer, or in whiting. This brightened up the surface, which could then be burnished by rubbing with polished steel or bloodstone. Experiments to improve the finish lead to the introduction of suphuret of carbon, which was dissolved into the silver solution in very small quantities. This ensured that the deposit of silver was much brighter, with a hard, metallic appearance after burnishing. Once polished, each piece was ready for dispatch to an eager public which never seemed to have had enough of the new wares.

Problems associated with Electroplate

The main problem for the manufacturers of electroplate was the health hazards faced by their employees. *The Application of Art to Manufactures* by George C. Mason and G. P. Putnam, published in 1858, describes the horrors suffered by a certain Mr Napier, a highly literate plate worker who gives 'his own experience, and that of his companions, while employed in electro-plating and gilding, in appartments that were improperly ventilated'. He first mentions ulcers, 'not only annoying but painful', which formed wherever the skin came into contact with the silver solution. Other side-effects were even more alarming, including 'a general languor of the body… a benumbing sensation in the head, with pains, not acute, shooting along the brow… bleeding at the nose in the morning… giddiness… momentary feelings as of the earth lifting up… feelings of terror, gloomy apprehensions, and irritability of temper. There follows a rushing of blood to the head; the rush is felt behind the ears with a kind of hissing noise, causing pain and blindness…' Although Mr Napier eventually gave up his unpleasant and highly dangerous occupation, he went on to say 'for months afterwards a dimness remained, as if a mist intervened between us and the object looked at'.

Reputable and successful companies like Elkington and Co. of Birmingham, or the Meriden Britannia Co. of Meriden, Connecticut, managed to avoid these problems by constructing well-designed and ventilated purpose-built premises. It is inevitable, however, that many smaller firms mistreated their workforce. Perhaps the worst offenders were the companies which transferred from the manufacture of fused plate in the mid-19th century. The new methods and techniques obviously involved a large initial outlay of money, as new tools and equipment were purchased. Their cash was largely tied up in redundant stock which no-one seemed to want at any price, and there was very little money left over for the well-being of the employees, who suffered greatly until factory health regulations were introduced, later in the century.

Perhaps the only problem faced by the buyers of electroplate was the speed at which it tarnished. The silver deposited by the new process was pure silver, and not the sterling standard used in the fused plate industry. Pure silver discolours far more rapidly than sterling silver, making frequent cleaning a necessity. However, one must remember that electroplate was never inexpensive. Joy D. Freeman considers the wages of labourers and artisans in the second half of the 19th century, comparing them with the prices charged for plated objects and concluding 'It wasn't the "rising" middle class who could afford silverplate, it was the "already risen" middle and upper classes… We can see that silverplate was not for the lower end of the economic scale. There was nothing cheap about silverplate – it was only available to the wealthy…' She reminds us, in the second part of her article, published in *Silver* magazine, of the huge numbers of immigrants who worked as domestic staff in 19th century America. Ill-equipped for other work due to language difficulties, they had to be content with low salaries and long working hours. In Britain, too, an enormous number of women served as domestic servants. Indeed *Useful Toil*, a book containing autobiographies of the working class from the 1820s to the 1920s, publishes tables showing that, up until the outbreak of the First World War in 1914, 'domestic service constituted the largest single employment for English women, and the second-largest employment for all English people, male and female'. The editor, John Burnett, quotes Samuel and Sarah Adams' *The Complete Servant*, published in 1825, giving an astonishing picture of how people on low incomes could afford at least one servant. In fact, the employment of domestic help was seen very much as a status symbol. Rowntree concluded, in his study of York, that the working classes ended at the level of the 'servant-keeping class' who employed a single 'skivvy' for heavy kitchen labour, and many families did without luxuries, rather than dispense with their over-worked, under-paid 'maids-of-all-work'. Thus, people of quite modest means had no need to worry about their plate tarnishing. Their servants were kept busy, often from dawn until late at night, ensuring that everything was kept sparklingly clean. Such rigorous treatment eventually wore away the thin silver skin, but then pieces could always be 'dipped' or re-plated. The worn plate was returned, as good as new, after a quick and inexpensive visit to the local jewellers or department store.

Early Electroplate

Electroplating base metals with gold was first carried out early in the 19th century, after the invention of the electric pile circa 1800 by Alessandro Volta, Professor of Physics at the University of Pavia. A contemporary, Luigi Galvani, experimented with the effects of electricity, lending his name to the term galvanism, used to describe early pieces of electroplate.

Other scientists carried out further experiments, and both William Cruickshank and Luigi Brugnatelli successfully gilded silver and base metal during the first few years of the 19th century. Needless to say, silver and goldsmiths were very interested in these developments, realising that the process had enormous potential. The Royal Goldsmiths Rundell, Bridge and Rundell manufactured a silver goblet, described in an inventory of 1832 as 'A very small Galvanic Goblet, with basso-relievo of the Hours'. Hallmarked in London in 1814, this rare piece, still in the royal collection, appears to be the earliest surviving object decorated with electroplating. A pair of unmarked parcel-gilt and silvered swan design candlesticks is illustrated on page 142. These are exact copies of a pair of parcel-gilt silver candlesticks made by Rundell, Bridge and Rundell and hallmarked in London in 1825. One can assume that these cheaper copies were produced almost simultaneously with their more expensive counterparts, dating to a period well before the normally accepted date of electroplate.

Other experiments were carried out in electrotyping, a process in which objects could be reproduced in the minutest detail by electrically depositing copper on to a plate submerged in solution. Developed in the 1830s, this process, sometimes called galvanoplastik, meant that exact copies could be 'grown' in the plating vat, without harming the original. Several scientists and metal workers succeeded in making medallions in this way. Their research was published in England in 1839, provoking much interest in the press.

A pair of unmarked 7in (17.8cm) electro parcel-gilt and silvered candlesticks by Rundell, Bridge and Rundell, c.1825. Extremely rare and early examples of electroplating, these could retail for as much as £4,000-£6,000.

A curious relic engraved: 'Mary Fox. Electro-Gilt by Elkington and Co. 1843'. This early piece of marked electro-gilt silver is actually a George III bowl, 'Victorianised' by later chasing. 7½in (19.1cm) diameter, it is only worth £200-£300, despite the interesting engraving. (See Marks, page 218)

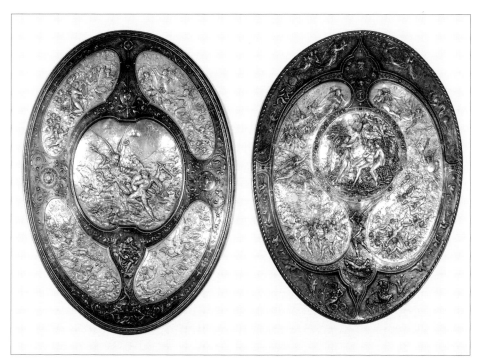

Two splendid electrotyped shields reproduced from originals sculpted by Leonard Morel-Ladeuil, one depicting Milton's Paradise Lost, *the other Bunyan's* Pilgrim's Progress. *The 34½in (87.6cm) Milton shield was well received by the press,* The Art Journal *reporting: 'the work...is the best...exhibited during the memorable year of 1867'. Shown at The Paris Universal Exhibition of 1868, the shield was awarded the gold medal. The piece was subsequently bought by The Victoria and Albert Museum, who authorised Elkington to produce copies for sale to the public and to art colleges. These copies cost 12 guineas each, in 1880. The Bunyan shield was exhibited at The Paris Exhibition of 1878, and was also purchased by the museum for study and copying purposes, the replicas costing 15 guineas. Today they would bring £2,000-£3,000 each.*

However, two Birmingham cousins, George Richard Elkington and Henry Elkington, were quick to see the industrial potential of these discoveries. They determined to concentrate all their efforts on obtaining as much control of the new processes as possible, buying up a great number of patents in both Britain and abroad, even when these seemed to be of little relevance to their trade. They also employed their potential rivals where possible, providing facilities for further experimentation to ensure that they had a monopoly of both present and future knowledge. Convinced that electroplating and electrotyping would revolutionise the plate industry, George Elkington started to construct a huge factory with showrooms in Newhall Street, Birmingham, as early as 1838, and by the early 1840s his company was producing large quantities of electroplated wares.

The manufacturers of Old Sheffield plate were secretly very concerned about the popularity of the new process, although many carried on as before, convinced that the public would soon tire of the novelty, returning to purchase fused plate when the Elkingtons went out of business. However, the cousins seemed to go from strength to strength, expanding their market to the great detriment of the fused plate industry. Moreover, as the Elkingtons owned the monopoly on electroplate, they were in a very powerful position. They were only prepared to share their techniques under very stringent conditions. First of all, they insisted that a down payment of £1,000 should be given, and that royalties should be paid on the weight of silver deposited, and then they also demanded that their marks be stamped on all electroplated goods, alongside the marks of the actual makers. Due to the lack of demand for fused plate wares, many companies were now very tempted, but few accepted the harsh conditions. After all, some had been in business for several

Henry Cole, first Director of the Victoria and Albert Museum, felt that one of the most important roles of the museum was to supply art schools with historic pieces for study purposes. Under his influence, Elkington signed an agreement with the Science and Art Department, afterwards producing many authorised replicas of precious silver objects from the collection. These were sold to the public and to newly-founded museums, such as The Metropolitan of New York. The majority bear an applied oval plaque, showing that they had been officially approved. Here we see a group of electrotyped replicas of 17th century and earlier silver objects, the largest 15in (38.1cm) tall. Sadly, in each case the oval mark has been defaced, presumably by someone who sought to pass the pieces off as originals. Perfect copies in every detail, today they are worth £400-£600 each.

decades, and their pride would simply not allow them to stamp the Elkingtons' marks, even if they could afford to pay the financial costs.

Although George Elkington soon reduced his financial demands and ceased to insist on his mark, he was still rebuffed by many manufacturers who firmly hoped that electroplating was a 'five minute wonder'. Samuel Roberts, officially retired but still a respected figure in the firm of Roberts, Smith and Co. of Sheffield, wrote to his nervous colleagues: 'I am persuaded that their mode of plating will inevitably be much less used than you are anticipating'. The firm followed his advice, almost certainly to their subsequent regret as, in May 1843, they were forced to cut their prices by fifty per cent, in a vain effort to attract back some of their erstwhile customers. This bold move achieved very little. The public had taken to the naturalistic designs impossible to reproduce in fused plate. Moreover, the Birmingham company was able to make and sell pieces far more cheaply than its rivals. Despite a brief moment of hopefulness aroused by the luke-warm praise afforded to the Elkingtons at The Great Exhibition of 1851, the fickle public refused to be tempted back to the more traditional methods of manufacture. As early as 1849 the *Tablet* had reported: 'Old families are turning their plate into this new security and some of the noblest names are among the patrons of the patentees', while the jury of the 1862 International Exhibition praised the 'advantages (of electroplate), now so generally admitted'. Fused plate was not even mentioned.

Eventually, Roberts, Smith and Co., along with all the other reluctant plate makers had to change their operations, adopting the Elkingtons' new techniques, or be forced into bankruptcy. Regrettably many delayed too long, and only just over one third of the well-known Sheffield companies survived into the middle of the 19th century.

An impressive American electroplated revolving cruet, by Rogers, Smith & Co. of Meriden, Connecticut, measuring no less than 17½in (44.5cm) high. Made c.1890, it is much more elaborate than its British contemporaries. Notice the aesthetic decoration featuring peacock feathers and the original bottles, crudely etched with foliage. £250-£350.

The Later Wares

Despite the misgivings of the fused plate manufacturers, electroplate became increasingly popular, and by the late 1850s it was well-established in Britain, America, and on the Continent. It is thought that the first maker to use electroplating in The United States was John O. Mead, a manufacturer of Britannia metal wares who came from Philadelphia. He certainly travelled to Britain to learn all about the Elkingtons' exciting new technique, returning after buying a battery so that he could carry out experiments of his own. By 1845 he was able to electroplate with great success, and he joined forces with silversmiths William and Asa Rogers. The partners, now based in Hartford, Connecticut, set up a short-lived concern, Rogers and Mead. They did not see eye to eye, and Mead soon left to return to Philadelphia, where he began trading under his own name. Meanwhile William and Asa Rogers, soon to be joined by another brother, Simeon, founded their own company in 1847.

An early newspaper advertisement depicts their State Street store, a plain neo-classical building. A man carrying a bundle is just leaving, his wheelbarrow parked outside ready for his heavy parcel. This charming detail is presumably meant to show how busy the company was. The text beneath the picture praises their wares: 'The Rogers Brothers…are now producing an entirely new and novel article in silverware. The first pieces were produced early this year. They are importing German silver spoons and forks, which by a new and unique process are coated with pure silver. This is an important discovery, as it is found that goods so treated have all the good qualities of solid silver and are really much stronger and practical for service. Wherever they have been shown they are easily sold…We predict for this enterprising firm a large measure of success, and shall await further developments with interest.'

Various members of the Rogers family, sometimes in partnership with other makers, worked in the electroplating business, and the picture is rather confusing. You can find a clear account in the Rainwaters' *American Silverplate*, an excellent work reprinted in 1988. Here the convolutions of the Rogers' family are explained in great detail, the Rainwaters concluding: 'The three Rogers brothers were all, at one time or another, associated with various concerns making silverplated goods. It was they, more than any others, who established the silverplating industry in this country.'

In the meantime, a nearby town, Meriden, was one of the centres for the manufacture of Britannia metal wares. This soft, grey metal, an alloy of tin hardened by small amounts of antimony and copper, had been greatly admired by the buying public and, in 1852, several small companies joined forces to become The Meriden Britannia Co., under the leadership of Horace and Dennis Wilcox. This conglomerate included workshops in Meriden, soon to be known as 'Silver City', and in neighbouring Wallingford. The board soon realised that the company could not operate efficiently with factories scattered around Connecticut, so purpose-built wooden three-storey premises were constructed in Meriden in 1856. By now the fickle public was becoming less and less interested in Britannia metal, preferring the new electroplated Rogers Brothers products. As a result, The Meriden Britannia Co.'s new premises included a small plating shop, which employed seventy-four workers. They were kept busy, electroplating the Britannia metal wares produced by their colleagues, in order to satisfy the public's wishes. Needless to say, they could not keep up with demand so, in July 1863, work began on a brick-built factory four storeys high, 500 feet long, and forty feet wide. Huge by 19th century standards, the completion of this factory ensured that the company could firmly establish itself as the leading manufacturer of both electroplate and Britannia metal in America. By now The Meriden Britannia Co. was by far the largest employer in the area, and its factory, known locally, with affection, as 'The Big Shop', could not satisfy their needs. As a result, in 1865, several houses were constructed in Park Street, Meriden. These were rented out to the employees, many of whom worked at home, burnishing the huge output of flatware. In the early days most pieces could still be bought in plain Britannia metal, optional electroplating adding about eighty per cent to the cost. Gradually, however, plated goods became increasingly important, as the company went from strength to strength, using a number of excellent marketing techniques to spread its fame throughout the United States and even abroad, establishing showrooms and offices in New York, San Francisco, Chicago and London. The latter office was very important, as it enabled the company to contact

South American and Australian retailers who spent huge sums of money. The company also produced catalogues illustrated with woodcuts, so that far-flung clients could still see their wares. The largest, of which no fewer than 30,000 copies were printed using over fifty tons of paper, was an impressive tome with over 3,200 illustrations of more than 300 classes of object ranging from the familiar to the very obscure. Some of these wares are illustrated later in this work, but can give only a taste of the extraordinary designs made in America in the last quarter of the 19th century. Each object had a code name so that orders could be telegraphed without delay or confusion, one word sufficing to describe each piece in the catalogue, in order to save both time and money.

The late 19th century heralded the start of a new era. Many of the manufacturers of plate had been operating at a net loss after a series of short economic slumps in 1893, 1894 and 1896. Even the seemingly all-powerful Meriden Britannia Co.'s sales had fallen from over $2 million to $1.5 million in 1894 and $1.4 million in 1896. The management realised that economies of scale had to be introduced, and in 1898 the company combined with no fewer than seventeen other firms to form a massive conglomerate, The International Silver Co. Cut-backs were made immediately, and twelve New York showrooms were reduced to three, while in Chicago the company was able to get rid of four independent retail outlets. Advertising was centralised, and some less popular lines were cancelled altogether. Despite these benefits, the new company did not make vast profits, and there were many criticisms that the public was faced with a virtual monopoly in the electroplate trade. Take-over bids and strikes also took their toll in the early part of this century. However, the company overcame all its problems, and became established as the world's largest producer of plated wares in the first quarter of the 20th century.

The British plate industry continued to be dominated by Elkington and Co. of Birmingham, although many Sheffield companies speedily adapted their factories to the output of electroplate. The city grew in size and importance, its population rising from 31,000 in 1800 to 380,000 in 1900. Birmingham grew at a similar rate, as more and more people were drawn in from the surrounding countryside to find work. Many were employed in the manufacture of electroplate, and both cities soon had a huge number of factories, large and small, which catered for the tremendous demand for plated goods. The majority were very old-fashioned by American standards and, as late as 1901, Ashbee, an important British Arts and Crafts designer, was most concerned, after visiting The Gorham Manufacturing Co. of Providence, Rhode Island. He commented 'that the application of machinery has been carried to such a pitch of excellence and precise skill in its use for the making of silver ware which no firm in England can come anywhere near... In England the great Silversmiths' houses are dying, they have not the capital nor the means nor the wits to put in the newest American machinery, nor the brains...'.

Britain, on the whole, never attempted to emulate the extraordinary designs so popular in 19th century America. The buying public tended to be far more conservative, so plate manufacturers contented themselves with making well-tried and tested styles, often copying shapes originally made in silver. Many were straightforward reproductions of 'antique' designs, although these were usually adapted until they had scarcely anything in common with their prototypes. Thus, one of the most popular pieces, the so-called 'Queen Anne' teasets with their part-fluted oval bodies, bear no resemblance whatsoever to any genuine early 18th century objects. In the 1880s, there was a reaction against conservatism. Dr.

An unusual parcel-gilt electrotype visiting card case by Elkington and Co. of Birmingham. Although this piece is only 3¾in (9.5cm) high, it is covered with detailed decoration including Medusa-like heads, flowers and foliage on textured grounds. £300-£400.

Christopher Dresser's bizarre designs started off a new trend for Arts and Crafts wares, hand-made pieces characterised by simplicity of form and strong, often linear, outline. However, the majority of people simply could not accept them in their pure form, and the stark, powerful pieces were bought by only a few of the avant-garde. Manufacturers soon plagiarised the designs of Dresser and his followers, producing toned-down versions for more general consumption.

Mid-19th century and later electroplate has become extremely popular over the last few years. Admirers of Dresser's pieces have to pay large sums for his wares, especially if they are impressed with facsimiles of the doctor's signature, while sentimental, naturalistic objects also attract high prices, particularly in America. The demand for electroplate is still growing, as more and more young collectors are attracted to the relatively new field. Museums are also purchasing the more unusual objects, and so it seems likely that costs will continue to soar for many years to come.

An attractive pair of 12½in (31.8cm) electroplated candlesticks by Elkington and Co. of Birmingham, with the date letter for 1885. This classical style has been popular since the 1770s, and is still much reproduced today, the modern copies usually of poor quality, with badly-cast mounts and coarse flutes on the columns.
£400-£600.

Candlesticks and Candelabra

In the mid-19th century candlesticks and candelabra, along with primitive oil lamps, were still the only method of lighting in many homes but were soon replaced by gas and electricity, and with cleaner, more sophisticated oil lamps. Nevertheless, they continued to be manufactured in large numbers, many people preferring the subtle and flattering glow of candles to the more useful but harsh and cold light provided by up-to-date methods. Dinner parties were still illuminated by huge candelabra, many almost smothered with cast and applied naturalistic decoration, and the majority of people still carried chamber candlesticks to light their way upstairs to bed, as both gas and electricity were, at first, usually confined to the ground floor. There has been a revival of interest in candlelight, as we seek to combat the stresses of modern life, creating relaxing ambiances as far removed as possible from present day offices and factories, usually over-bright with neon lighting. As a result, prices for plated candlesticks and candelabra have soared, quite ordinary examples retailing for a minimum of £200.

Electroplate was also used a great deal in the manufacture of oil lamp bases, many later converted to electricity once the new form of lighting was well-established. Later still, purpose-built electroplated table lamps were produced in large quantities. Plated oil and electric lamps are still in great demand, often selling for several hundreds of pounds at auction.

Three mid-19th century candelabra, the tallest 30in (76.2cm) high, one with interchangeable sconces and gilt bonbon dishes. The cast human and animal figures applied to the rockwork bases are of excellent quality, with finely modelled details. The central example is unmarked, while the two outer specimens were both made by Elkington and Co. Left to right: £1,500-£2,000, £800-£1,000, £1,500-£2,000.

An attractive 36in (91.4cm) five-light candelabrum dating to c.1870, once again made by Elkington and Co. Applied with numerous cast mounts and with a charming vase of flowers finial, this single piece could sell for £1,000-£1,200.

An unusual set of eight unmarked 10½in (26.7cm) candlesticks dating from the mid-19th century, their baluster forms an adaptation of a style popular one hundred years earlier. Engraved with arabesques, and still with all their original nozzles, these would now retail for £1,500-£2,000, although one could still find a similar pair for £250-£300. These are much more expensive as it is very rare to find such a large number of matching candlesticks.

A pair of unmarked 18in (45.7cm) candlesticks with plated nickel stems and Britannia metal bases. Heavily-applied with cast trailing vine mounts, they probably date from the last quarter of the 19th century. Although rather too tall for many homes, they would still sell for £250-£300, as candlesticks of all shapes and sizes are currently very popular.

An unusual novelty 6½in (16.5cm) chamberstick, perhaps a little macabre for today's tastes. Great numbers of items were fashioned from the hooves of favourite horses and ponies and, although few are marked, they are often conveniently engraved with the date of the poor beast's death. This particular example had a date: 'July 19, 1872'. £150-£200.

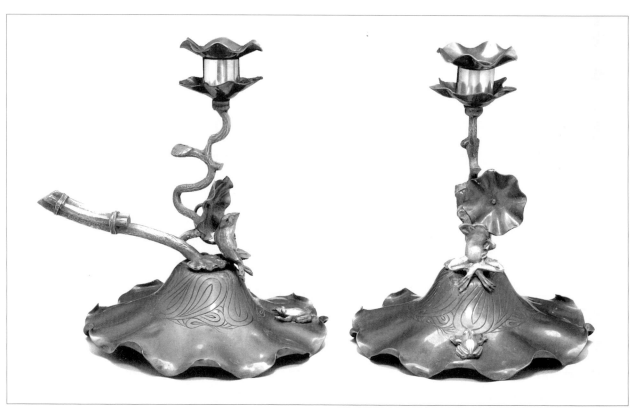

A splendid pair of unmarked American mixed metals chambersticks dating from the last quarter of the 19th century. Their bases, drip pans and nozzles, and the flower-shaped mounts are made of copper decorated with pink enamelling, while the other parts are made of electro-plate. Just over 7in (17.8cm) tall, they are each applied with two amusing cast, plated frogs. Novelty pieces are very popular today, and these could retail for as much as £600-£800, even though they are very worn.

A pair of charming unmarked 8½in (21.6cm) wall sconces inset with Wedgwood style jasperware pottery plaques. Highly decorative and yet small enough for display in the most modest home, these were made c.1880. £600-800. They are illustrated with an unmarked woven wire beehive honeypot applied with a cast honey bee. Typical of the whimsical nature of many mid-19th century artefacts, this delightful piece might sell for £400-£600.

A 9in (22.9cm) high cockerel inkstand made of electroplated brass, a material ideal for casting with such fine detail. Unmarked, it probably dates from the last half of the 19th century. £300- £500. The 5in (12.7cm) electroplated copper candlesticks are also 19th century, dating from c.1890, although their design would suggest an earlier Regency date. The copper, exposed by years of cleaning, could easily lead an unsuspecting buyer to assume that they are made of Old Sheffield plate. £150-£200.

An impressive pair of unmarked 21in (53.3cm) oil lamps applied with electrotyped friezes of classical figures. Each lamp lifts off its pedestal base, reducing the height by almost a third. The opaque glass globes transfer-printed with fox-hunting scenes are later, dating from this century, while the lamps themselves were made c.1870. £2,000-£2,500 the pair. They are illustrated with an unmarked electro-plated tea urn made in the neo-classical style of the 1770s, but actually manufactured about one hundred years later. £700-£1,000.

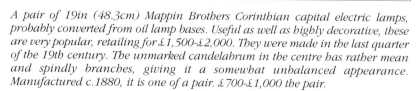

A pair of 19in (48.3cm) Mappin Brothers Corinthian capital electric lamps, probably converted from oil lamp bases. Useful as well as highly decorative, these are very popular, retailing for £1,500-£2,000. They were made in the last quarter of the 19th century. The unmarked candelabrum in the centre has rather mean and spindly branches, giving it a somewhat unbalanced appearance. Manufactured c.1880, it is one of a pair. £700-£1,000 the pair.

An attractive but badly worn 20in (50.8cm) Art Nouveau table lamp made from electroplated spelter, a brittle zinc alloy. Spelter objects are usually quite inexpensive, as the metal breaks so easily. Nevertheless, pieces made in the Art Nouveau period are very fashionable, so this unmarked lamp could retail for £600-£800, once replated.

Dining Plate

Traditional dining room pieces, such as soup tureens, platters and centrepieces, continued to be manufactured in huge numbers throughout the second half of the 19th century and well into the 20th century. Fashions still dictated that formal meals with many courses were served, even if the family was dining alone. However, designs altered drastically, with the introduction of the newly fashionable naturalistic decoration which swept both Britain and America into a frenzy. Some extraordinary pieces were created, some so bizarrely decorated that their basic function almost disappeared beneath a mass of applied plant forms.

The advent of electroplate also saw the introduction of a whole host of new objects, used for the first time in the mid-19th century, when the well-to-do amassed an enormous range of plate. To quote Joy D. Freeman, in the November 1986 issue of *Silver* magazine: 'Having someone to polish the silver, dust the furniture, and keep the house shining enabled the lady of the house to occupy herself with social etiquette, including her concern for possessing the right serving pieces. There were berry spoons, which were not to be used for any other fruit. There were olive spoons, lettuce forks, and tomato servers; special jars for pickles (and special tongs to go with them), nut bowls decorated with perched squirrels, syrup jugs, sardine boxes… cream and sugar sets just for after dinner fruits, lobster shell dishes with a very realistic lobster stretched across the top, and many other one-use-only pieces. Each member of the family had an individual napkin ring embellished with figures, animals, wheeled carts, flower vases, salt-and-pepper and butter pat holders, or any

One of a set of five graduated meat dish covers, the largest 19½in (49.5cm) long. Applied with cast gadroon mounts, and with detailed cast handles, they were made by Mappin and Webb of Sheffield in the last quarter of the 19th century (see page 218). £1,000-£1,200 the set, although individual electroplated dish covers can still be found for less than £150.

An American electroplated soup tureen made by the Southington Plate Co. prior to 1893, when the firm was bought out by the Meriden Britannia Company. It is also marked 'Quadruple Plate', implying that the silver coating was four times thicker than usual. 10¾in (27.3cm) long, this sturdy and useful piece would find a ready market today, particularly in the USA. £400-£600.

Two late 19th century biscuit barrels with electroplated mounts, the glass example with enamelled decoration by Elkington and Co. of Birmingham, the carved oak example unmarked. Today both would make ideal ice buckets, the wooden specimen inset with a pottery liner to contain the water. They are 9½in (24.1cm) and 8½in (21.6cm) tall. £400-£600 and £200-£250.

A 20¼in (51.4cm) electrotype sideboard dish designed by Morel-Ladeuil and produced by Elkington and Co. of Birmingham, the original sculpted in 1876. The electrotype process enabled many exact copies to be produced and marketed on a worldwide basis. As a result, this piece is engraved 'Design copyrighted in the United States November 1876' and with similar sentiments protecting the company in France, Germany and the Austro-Hungarian Empire. £1,000-£1,500.

An unmarked late 19th/early 20th century electroplated egg cruet, its simple shape and crimped border based loosely on the designs of Dr Christopher Dresser, the avant-garde designer. Note that the egg cups themselves are lined with gilding, serving to protect the metal from the sulphur in the eggs. The 8in (20.3cm) piece even has tiny slots designed to hold the egg spoons, although these are now missing. £150-£200.

An American early 20th century 22in (55.9cm) platter of traditional shape, moulded with a gravy well and tree, and with an inscription recording that it was presented in 1910. This piece was made by Tiffany and Co., of New York, and has a very detailed mark (see page 218). Sadly, it is badly scratched, and the inscription would deter most buyers, hence £150-£200.

combination of these.' The list seems endless, and one can add cracker trays and boxes, known in Britain as biscuit barrels, biscuit warmers, bonbon dishes and flower vases, revolving-top breakfast dishes, spoon warmers, egg coddlers, and a wide range of novelty cruets. One wonders how many of these wonderful objects were actually used on a regular basis. Now, after many years of scorn, they are again in great demand, selling remarkably well in Britain, and even better in the USA.

There was a reaction against these splendid creations later in the century, and more simple, severe styles were introduced. This trend was encouraged, early in the 20th century, by the horrors of the First World War. Dining on such a grand scale became unthinkable, and small, intimate supper parties became extremely popular. When the war was over, very few people could afford to go back to their lavish lifestyles. The working classes had experienced more lucrative occupations, many women toiling in munitions' factories where they were not only able to earn more money, but also their free time was their own. Few were willing to return to the constricting duties of domestic service, so the wealthy were deprived of their armies of cleaners and maids. As a result, much plate was relegated to storerooms, where it languished, often in perfect condition, until rediscovered a few years ago. Fortunately, there now seems to be an ever increasing demand for good electroplate, the market swallowing up items of quality or of unusual design. Prices are still soaring, and there seems to be no danger that the public will tire of old electroplate.

An attractive suite of three unmarked dessert stands inscribed and dated 1875, each still with its original engraved glass fruit bowl. Complete sets in good condition are now very scarce, retailing for £2,000-£3,000. Here, the tallest example is 24½in (62.2cm) high.

A small centrepiece applied with a cast biblical figure, a choice of decoration which seems curious today, although one must remember that many of our 19th century ancestors were deeply religious. Made by Elkington and Co., and clearly marked on the socle base, it is 18in (45.7cm) tall. Today it would retail for £300-£400, a low price reflecting the missing bowl plus the religious subject, a little too severe for modern tastes.

A splendid 9½in (24.1cm) centrepiece engraved with several diamond registration marks for March, 1876. The rockwork base is applied with two cast walruses, while the stem is encrusted with icicles. The vendor of this piece suggested that it was made for presentation to a man named White, who helped to organise the disastrous Polar Expedition of 1875, led by Captain Nares. It sold, in June 1989, for £700 plus 10% premium. It would now retail for at least £1,200-£1,500.

This dainty electroplated oil and vinegar cruet is engraved with a retailer's name: 'Asprey, London'. 7¼in (18.4cm) high and fitted with finely cut glass bottles, it is both of excellent quality and a pleasingly simple design. £150-£200.

Here we see a 19th century egg cruet originally fitted with six egg cups. The boiled eggs are kept warm inside the cruet, the sides opening as the central lid is turned. Made of electroplated Britannia metal but unmarked, this 10½in (26.7cm) piece proved difficult to sell, as one of the cups was missing. £200-£300.

This late Victorian biscuit barrel combines electroplate and cut glass most attractively, although the yellow tones of the metal mean that this piece requires replating. It is stamped with an unidentified maker's mark, N.C. and Co., and is 8½in (21.6cm) wide. £400-£600.

A late 19th century American dessert stand by The Meriden Britannia Co., applied with cast cherubs and a winged classical figure, although the base and the feet reflect the Egyptianesque styles so popular at this time. 25in (63.5cm) tall, it would now sell for £1,000-£1,200. The piece, fitted with engraved glass bonbon dishes, is illustrated in the reprinted 1886-87 catalogue, priced at $110.

A simple, elegant 15in (38.1cm) centrepiece by Mappin and Webb, the clear glass vases shading into pink. It was made at the turn of the century, when people had already started to entertain on a less grand scale. Dainty enough to appeal to buyers with smaller homes, it would now retail for £400-£600.

A good late Victorian 14½in (36.8cm) soup tureen with matching ladle, each applied with well modelled cast details. Notice that the imaginative engraver has skilfully followed the naturalistic theme when executing the monogram, forming the entwined letters from sprouting twigs. Made by Walker and Hall, this would sell for £1,200-£1,600.

An 8in (20.3cm) high soup tureen designed by Dr. Christopher Dresser and impressed with a patent registration mark for 1880. This piece was made by Hukin and Heath, a Birmingham partnership which manufactured many of Dresser's designs. £4,000-£6,000, as it does not bear the all-important facsimile signature of Dr. Dresser.

A 9in (22.9cm) cauldron-shaped soup tureen loosely copying the previous piece. In fact this tureen is weak and subdued, the manufacturer toning down Dresser's extraordinary design to produce an uncontroversial alternative for its middle class, conservative customers. Made by Henry Wilkinson and Co. (see page 218), c.1890, it would now cost £400-£600.

Two Victorian cruets and an egg cruet, the largest almost 12in (30.5cm) high. Each is stamped: 'E.P.N.S.', but has no maker's mark. Cruets fitted with perfect cut-glass bottles are now very popular, although the smallest chips reduce the value considerably. Left to right: c.1870, £200-£250; c.1890, £120-£160; c.1870, £200-£250.

Novelty cruets sell very well, both here and in the USA. Here we see an 8in (20.3cm) rocking horse example with untraced maker's mark. Unfortunately the glass salt cellar is missing, and the piece is badly worn and pitted. £300-£400 if restored. It is illustrated with an Elkington and Co. electrotyped table bell c.1880, modelled as an old woman, the figure nodding her head almost reprovingly as the bell rings. £300-£400.

An amusing unmarked 7in (17.8cm) cruet c.1880, modelled as a pump, pail and milk churn, its base engraved to simulate paving stones. This rare piece would now retail for £400-£600.

One of a pair of 6½in (16.5cm) basket-shaped wire cruets applied with cast chicks and with egg-shaped condiments. Notice the original spoons, their terminals cast with ears of corn. Made by Mappin and Webb and impressed with the diamond registration mark for 1867 (see page 219), these might sell for £300-£400 the pair, as they are in very poor condition.

Three novelty bonbon dishes dating from the mid- to late 19th century, all with unidentified makers' marks. The 9in (22.9cm) double shell example on the left is made from electroplated nickel although the stag is cast in Britannia metal. Fitted with frosted glass liners, it may have been used as a butter or preserve dish. Left to right: £150-£200, £70-£100, and £100-£120.

An American late 19th century 10in (25.4cm) cake basket chased with fruiting branches. Made by Pairpoint of New Bedford, this attractive piece would sell for £300-£400.

Complicated in design, this American 14½in (36.8cm) compote is applied with alternating male and female classical masks, a fox and a humming bird. It was made by Reed and Barton of Taunton c.1880. £300-£500.

An unmarked 9in (22.9cm) Britannia metal vase c.1890, applied with brass feet, beaded rim and nautical details, the theme continued with an engraved vignette of two yachts. Obviously, when new, it was entirely covered with silver, so the two metals used in its construction would not have been visible. This piece, probably designed as a sporting trophy, has been cleaned until hardly any silver plating remains. Nevertheless its shipping motifs would appeal to collectors of nautical artefacts, so it could retail for as much as £200-£300, despite its poor condition.

An attractive woven wire bread or cake basket about 12in (30.5cm) in diameter, applied with well-modelled, cast ears of corn and engraved with an elaborate cartouche. Clearly stamped 'E.P.' and with an unidentified maker's initials (see page 219), it was manufactured c.1880. £300-£400.

A Britannia metal 11in (27.9cm) Japanese-style baluster vase enriched with several different colours of gilding and with a chemically induced patination implying great antiquity. In fact, it was manufactured by The Meriden Britannia Co c.1880. £300-£400.

An American aesthetic taste 13½in (34.3cm) vase, the plated stand modelled with Japanese fans, kites and bamboo leaves. The blue glass vase is, somewhat incongruously, enamelled in white with a Kate Greenaway style little boy. Miss Greenaway's delightful subjects were frequently used by American silversmiths, who produced a host of charmingly sentimental objects decorated with children in early Victorian period costume. This piece was made by Rogers and Brother of Waterbury and dates to c.1875. £600-£800.

Some vases were designed to hold celery rather than flowers. This American example, by Reed and Barton of Taunton, is fitted with a part-frosted glass container finely cut with a foliate frieze. Almost 9in (22.9cm) high, it was made in the last quarter of the 19th century. £180-£220.

Ovoid revolving-top breakfast dishes were very popular in the 19th century. Used for country house breakfasts when the guests were expected to help themselves, they contained bacon and kidneys. The food was kept warm by hot water, placed inside the bottom part of the dish. Complete specimens should contain two liners, one pierced to allow the bacon fat to drain away, the other solid, to prevent the drips of grease from intermingling with the hot water. Plain examples now sell for £400-£600, but this is more decorative than most, so could bring £600-£800. Made by Elkington and Co., c.1870, it is 14½in (36.8cm) long.

Above and above right: *A late 19th century 9½in (24.1cm) shell-fluted biscuit warmer by James Dixon and Sons of Sheffield (see page 219). The two lids drop down to reveal compartments with hinged, pierced covers. Hot biscuits or muffins were stored inside the closed compartments and placed before an open fire, ensuring that the contents maintained their warmth These spectacular pieces are now so popular they are being reproduced. Luckily modern copies are easily recognisable, as their cast handles and feet lack the crisp detail of the originals. £600-£800.*

Possibly unique, this 9in (22.9cm) biscuit barrel is modelled as a typical mid-Victorian town house, with bay windows and simulated fancy crested ridge tiles. Notice the engraved details such as the Venetian blinds and the bedroom curtains. Unmarked, it may have been made as an apprentice piece, or by a plate worker in his spare time. It is amusing to speculate that the maker may have used his own home as a model for this splendid object. £2,000-£3,000.

The Victorians loved the combination of plate and cut-glass, exemplified by this 11in (27.9cm) biscuit barrel made by Martin Hall and Co. of Sheffield, c.1870. The mounts are deliberately restrained, to show the lavishly star-cut brilliant glass off to its best advantage. £400-£500.

A group of American late 19th century small table ornaments, the vase only 8in (20.3cm) high. Figural pieces sell particularly well today, their somewhat naïve charm greatly appreciated by the sophisticated modern buyer. Left to right: Toothpick holder by Aurora, of Aurora, Illinois, £100-£150; bud vase by Simpson, Hall and Miller, of Wallingford, Connecticut, £70-£100; cream jug by The Meriden Britannia Plate Co., of Meriden, Connecticut, £70-£100; napkin ring by Wilcox, of Meriden, Connecticut, £70-£100.

Three late 19th century egg boilers with tiny spirit lamps. The outline of the 8½in (21.6cm) example on the left is reminiscent of Dr. Christopher Dresser's designs, so this would sell better than the other two, at £300-£400. The more ordinary specimens would realise £150-£200 each. All are unmarked.

Spoon warmers were usually modelled as nautilus shells. They were filled with hot water, the serving spoons or ladles placed inside, to warm their bowls. This scarce 8½in (21.6cm) specimen by Mappin Brothers of Sheffield in the shape of a stylised mandarin duck, c.1870, would now sell for £350-£450, although one can still find shell-shaped spoon warmers for £150-£200.

A 'gypsy cauldron', 18in (45.7cm) tall, with 'rustic' crossed twigs supporting a pan above a spirit lamp. Probably used to keep sauces or gravy hot, although some collectors argue that they are brandy pans or egg boilers. Made by James Dixon and Sons of Sheffield, c.1875, it is amusing enough to fetch £400-£500.

An amusing Meriden Britannia Co. 11in (27.9cm) nut bowl made c.1880, modelled as a half-eaten nut, with lily pad base, a cast squirrel perched cheekily on top. Typical of whimsical Victorian taste, this would have been scorned until quite recently. Today, objects like this are avidly sought , and it would retail for at least £400-£600.

An unmarked 36in (91.4cm) salmon dish inset with a removable teak platter. Well-modelled, this piece is comparatively recent, probably dating from the 1940s. As a result it should cost no more than £400-£600.

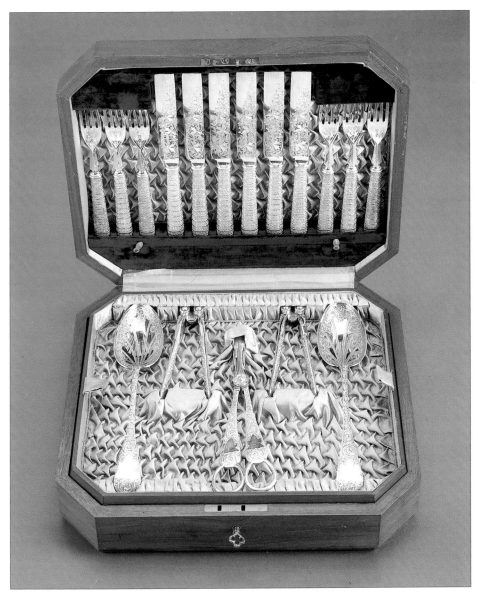

Left and overleaf: *This splendid electroplated dessert set including grape shears and nut crackers was made by Roberts and Belk of Sheffield, c.1900. Like so many similar sets, it was probably given as a wedding present and then hardly used by the recipients. The plush and satin linings are spotless and both the inlaid mahogany case and the contents are in perfect condition, thus making this comprehensive set an ideal gift today. £600-£800.*

Cutlery

The advent of electroplate meant that a huge amount of inexpensive but hard-wearing cutlery could be produced, in a large number of styles ranging from the traditional to more adventurous patterns. Naturalistic designs became very popular, some pieces so heavily moulded with flowers and leaves that they are difficult to use. Canteens with twelve or more place settings were advertised, the more extensive containing a number of pieces which one would no longer use. The United States seemed to lay great emphasis on 'the right tool for the right job', and the 19th century American housewife could set her table with an enormous range of cutlery, designed specially to cope with various foodstuffs. Edmund P. Hogan's *The Elegance of Old Silverplate* lists some of the more obscure pieces as follows: 'Chocolate muddler, cracker spoon, ice spoon, pea spoon, seven kinds of ladles, bottle opener, lobster pick, asparagus tongs, roast holder, poultry shears' and there were many others, such as macaroni forks, cold meat forks, orange spoons, pickle spoons, olive spoons, and a vast assortment of serving slices and spoons. British canteens are usually far less comprehensive however, most containing only quite basic eating and serving implements.

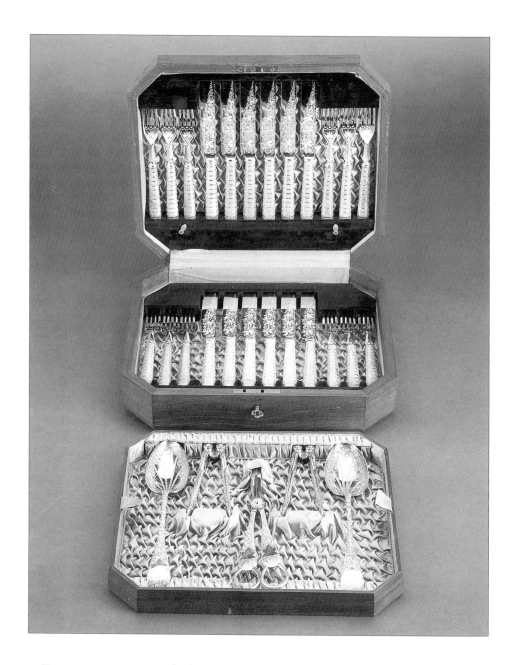

Enormous quantities of plated flatware were manufactured and the majority, often still in excellent condition, can be found very cheaply, especially in Britain. American collectors are far more interested in 19th and early 20th century plated flatware, paying large sums for unusual pieces in obscure patterns. Many are advertised in the bimonthly magazine *Silver*, by specialist dealers who help their customers to complete canteens of cutlery in a certain pattern. When I visited Meriden, the 'Silver City', in 1990, I was quite amazed by the prices asked for plated cutlery. Obviously the pieces in question are very rare, but nevertheless over $100 seemed a lot to pay for a set of six forks or spoons. In Britain one can still find odd half dozens for a few pounds, although complete canteens for twelve may cost several hundreds of pounds.

It is worth remembering that old electroplated flatware is of better quality than many of the modern services. The latter seem so bright when you purchase them, but the plating is often very thin. After a few years of use they are worn out, and have to be replated. Despite its age, turn-of-the-century plated flatware is often still in excellent condition, representing a much better buy.

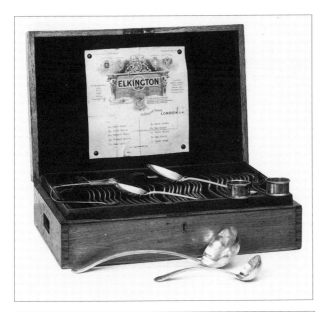

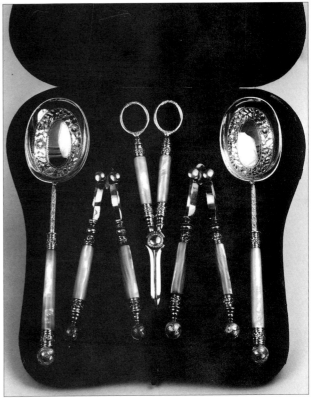

Above: *Dating from the late 19th century, this Martin Hall and Co. dessert set is made from plated steel and nickel silver, with pleasing mother-of-pearl handle mounts. (See Marks, page 219.) It is still in pristine condition, any damage prevented by the original plush-lined leather case, and so it would make an unusual gift today, hence £250-£300.*

Above left: *A late Victorian twelve place setting service of beaded flatware in its original baize-lined oak canteen. Notice the printed label proudly declaring: 'Elkington and Co. Ltd. Originators of Electro-plate'. Most turn-of-the-century canteens were so heavily plated that they are far more hard-wearing than their modern equivalents. They are, I feel, still underpriced. £700-£1,000.*

Standard fish slices and forks are still commonly available, normally retailing for £60-£100, even in their original fitted case. Novelty examples are much scarcer however, and one might have to pay £300-£400 for this pair, fashioned as a gardening spade and fork. Unmarked and c.1890, they have well carved wooden handles. The 'spade' is 11in (27.9cm) long.

A splendid Victorian electroplated Britannia metal coffee pot with well modelled cast feet, handle and finial, and with attractive engraved foliage surrounding vacant cartouches. 10½in (26.7cm) high, it was made by James Dixon and Sons c.1860. £200-£300.

Tea and Coffee Accessories

The style of tea and coffee accessories changed enormously in the mid-19th century, with the introduction of electroplate. Although no new objects appeared, new shapes were introduced along with new methods of decorating, creating a wealth of naturalistic, classical revival, Japanese-style, and Art Nouveau designs. Items were often much larger, too. One wonders if they were made mainly for display purposes, rather than for actual use. Certainly Joy D. Freeman writes: 'The quintessential symbol of the upper middle class during the second half of the 19th century was the elaborate, long-legged teaset with its numerous pieces decorating the sideboard'. Huge and impressive, the American Victorian teaset can be a total joy, although some, in my opinion, go too far, becoming rather vulgar. American sets were more complete than most British sets. They were usually sold with several extras such as waste bowls, preserve jars and butter dishes, the latter sometimes fitted with a small bell so that the lady of the house could summon the maid without leaving her guests. Until quite recently these spectacular tea and coffee sets were scorned by collectors of antiques. Now, however, they are in great demand, regularly selling for £1,000 to £1,500.

Tea kettles and urns continued to be manufactured well into the 20th century, as wealthy women were still able to enjoy much leisure time, spending many hours on social calls to friends and acquaintances. The large-scale emancipation of women,

Two pieces of late 19th/early 20th century electroplate, the 9½in (24.1cm) kettle unmarked, the 12in (30.5cm) salver engraved with a retailer's name and address, 'W. Marshall and Co., 134 Princess Street, Edinburgh', but no maker's mark. A great deal of electroplate was sold to the trade unmarked, retailers adding their own details before selling to the public. £200-£300 and £150-£200.

resulting more from the changes wrought by the First World War than by pressure from a few 'eccentrics', changed all this. Servants were no longer readily available, so middle class housewives had to spend more time on domestic chores. Even the very rich had become discontent with the tedium of afternoon visits. Many wealthy girls looked for careers, or started to travel, avoiding the boredom of waiting at home for a potential husband to appear. As a result, kettles and urns for domestic use were rarely manufactured after the 1920s, although some huge examples were made for commercial venues or for hire for functions, such as weddings. Today few people would dream of using a tea kettle or urn. Nevertheless, they are very saleable, good, attractive examples retailing for £500-£700. Highly ornamental, they are now used in a purely decorative role, gracing any home which is big enough to cope with such large pieces.

Part of a three-piece set, this American late 19th century teapot is made principally of Britannia metal, although the handle and finial are cast in nickel silver. Applied with cast mounts and chased with rather mean arabesques, the set was manufactured by The Meriden Britannia Co. c.1880. (See Marks, page 219.) The teapot is 7½in (19.1cm) high. £220-£280.

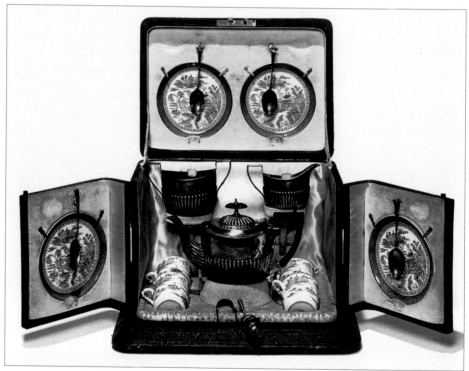

A standard 'Queen Anne' three-piece teaset by James Dixon and Sons, c.1890. Many thousands of tea and coffee sets were made in this style. It is typical of the late Victorian and Edwardian eras and actually owes nothing whatsoever to the designs of the early 18th century. This set, the teapot 6½in (16.5cm) high, is unusual, as it comes complete with a Staffordshire pottery teaset transfer-printed in the familiar 'Willow pattern'. There is even a set of teaspoons with a matching sugar spoon and a pair of sugar tongs. Still in its fitted case, it might retail for £600-£800, although one can still find a similar three-piece teaset with no extras for as little as £150-£200.

A comprehensive American seven-piece tea and coffee set, of the type mentioned by Joy D. Freeman. It has a covered preserve pot and a waste bowl, as well as two sugar basins, all features which are rarely found in British plated teasets. Made by Rogers, Smith and Co. of New Haven, c.1875, this attractive set has a matted finish engraved with flowers and leaves. It is large and imposing, the coffee pot almost 11in (27.9cm) high. 1,000-£1,500.

An unmarked American late 19th century tea and coffee service, the coffee pot 11in (27.9cm) tall. It is decorated with Japanese-style flowerheads and has nickel silver finials and feet, although the bodies are made from plated Britannia metal. This five-piece set would sell for £500-£700.

This fine quality coffee set was made by Tiffany and Co. of New York, c.1900. It is worth noting that tea and coffee sets designed for the British market rarely included lidded sugar bowls, a feature of both continental and American wares. The coffee pot is 7¾in (19.7cm) tall. £300-£500.

A more simple American tea and coffee service, the plain tapering oval bodies enlivened by Japanese-style engraved foliage within curiously-shaped panels. Notice the applied friezes die-rolled with birds, animals and insects. This Meriden Britannia Co. set, the coffee pot 9in (22.9cm) tall, probably dates from the very end of the 19th century. £400-£600.

Three late 19th/early 20th century swing-handled sugar baskets decorated with machine piercing, all unmarked. While 18th century examples were invariably fitted with 'Bristol' blue glass liners, later specimens might have a range of colours, as can be seen here. The basket in the centre is 7in (17.8cm) high. £60-£100 each.

A charming plated nickel afternoon teaset complete with a 9½in (24.1cm) kettle on stand and with sugar tongs, each piece engraved in the aesthetic taste with fans, blossoms and birds. The 'rustic' bark-textured details are unusual. Made by Martin Hall and Co. of Sheffield, c.1875, this might bring £400-£600.

A sturdy tea and coffee set made of Britannia metal decorated with engine-turning. Made by Walter Sperrier and Co. of Sheffield, it dates to c.1880. (See Marks, page 219.) Somewhat worn, it is also engraved with monograms. Both these factors would deter many potential buyers, hence £200-£300. The coffee pot is 10½in (26.7cm) tall.

Art Deco plate is highly collected, and this stylish geometric four-piece teaset, by the Adie Brothers of Sheffield, could sell for as much as £2,500-£3,000. Designed by Harold Stabler and made c.1920, it comes complete with a 12½in (31.8cm) bakelite tray.

Two unmarked mid-19th century tea kettles, the tallest almost 17½in (44.5cm) high. Although somewhat impractical today, they are most impressive, selling well as they are extremely decorative. The example on the left has an inscription dated 1858. £400-£600 each.

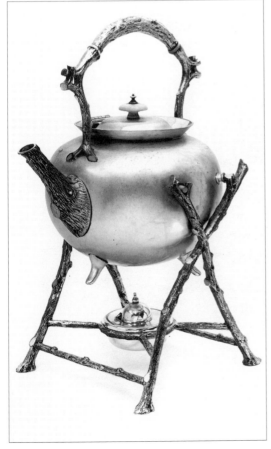

A mid-Victorian 'gypsy' tea kettle on a 'rustic' crossed twig stand. Manufactured by Martin Hall and Co. c.1860, this unusual piece is 14½in (36.8cm) high. £350-£450.

Three Victorian electroplated tea trays, the largest 28¼in (71.8cm) wide. Note that the top one is badly worn, the expense of replating adding substantially to the price. Gallery trays, less popular than their flat equivalents, can often be found for a third of the price, probably because of the quantity of poor quality reproductions on the market. £500-£700, £700-£1,000 and £400-£600.

A wonderfully detailed electroplated cake basket made c.1880 and 8¼in (21cm) long. Although of basic plain oval form, this splendid piece is enlivened by the addition of cast tassels and rope-twist borders, which lift it above the ordinary. Unmarked, it may well be of American manufacture. £250-£300.

An unusual 18in (45.7cm) tea-urn which works on the syphon principle. As hot water is drawn off, cold water is sucked through the tube from the open container. One can then add more cold water without the risk of burning or scalding oneself. Made by James Dixon and Sons of Sheffield c.1880, it bears their impressed bugle trademark. £600-£800.

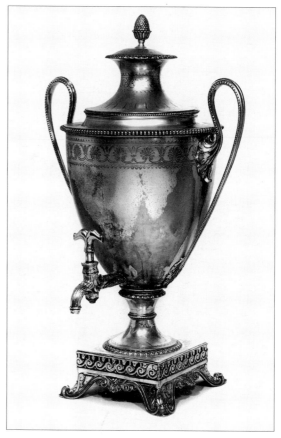

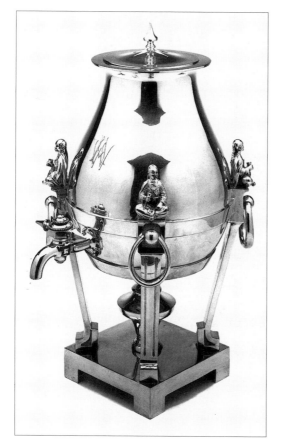

Above left: *A curious unmarked 17in (43.2cm) tea kettle with plated nickel stand and mounts, made c.1890. It has a continental pottery body painted in rich blue and iron red, with gilt enrichment. The pattern is derived from so called 'Derby Imari' porcelain, but this piece is of poor quality, with muddy colours and no fine detail. Still attractive from a distance, but sadly the spout is broken. A skilful silversmith could mask this quite easily by adding a metal tip, and the piece might then sell for £300-£400.*

Above: *In Victorian times the tea-urn was still considered indispensable for formal, 'at home' afternoons, when many friends were expected to call. This unmarked 22in (55.9cm) specimen reproduces a Georgian neo-classical design, although the original would have been smaller and more delicate. It is badly worn, but would still sell for £500-£700, as large examples of Victorian plate are in great demand as sideboard ornaments.*

An unmarked American mid- to late 19th century tea-urn applied with cast Chinese figures. Simple in design, it is 16½in (41.9cm) tall. The monogram would deter many buyers, so it would probably cost £500-£700.

An attractive Art Nouveau sugar and cream set on a 7½in (19.1cm) stand, the tendril handles applied with tiny flowerheads. Made by Hukin and Heath of Birmingham c.1890, this small piece is stylish and well-designed. Art Nouveau plate is very popular with the modern buyer, who might expect to pay £180-£220 for a similar set.

A selection of plated items with blue glass liners or pottery fittings. The 10in (25.4cm) Britannia metal preserve stand has two Spode 'Italian pattern' transfer-printed dishes. Although quite worn, it could still retail for £200-£250. The sugar and cream, pierced and die-stamped with arabesques, would sell for £70-£100, while the two French-style condiments might realise £100-£150. All are unmarked, and date from the late 19th or early 20th century.

A pair of Elkington and Co. 6in (15.2cm) tea caddies, decorated in the mid-18th century style with chased arabesques and with pagoda finials. Small caddies are tremendously popular, and this pair, one for black tea, the other for green tea, could realise £600-£800. They date from c.1870.

An unmarked plate-mounted oak tea caddy 12½in (31.8cm) long, probably made c.1890. Sturdy, and in good condition, though rather plain, it could sell for £500-£600.

Trays and Salvers

Once again, America led the field in the creation of splendid new designs, with Britain lagging far behind, sticking to long established, favourite patterns. Although one might imagine that the basic shape of a tray cannot be changed, one only needs to look at The Meriden Britannia Co. catalogues to see the vast array of wonderful styles offered to the 19th century buyer. 'Card receivers', small salvers which were placed on the hall table ready to hold the cards of visitors, were offered in no fewer than fifty-eight styles in the 1886 catalogue, a competing firm, Reed and Barton, providing another thirty-eight designs in 1885. Extremely ornamental, card receivers were applied with a host of cast details. To quote Dorothy T. and H. Ivan Rainwater, in an article from *Silver* magazine, October 1987, these might take the form of 'butterflies and other insects, owls, elephants, children and cherubs, swans, frogs, peacocks, storks, fruit, squirrels, cats, dogs, flowers, foliage in fantastic arrangements, and other animals, either *au naturel* or dressed in human garments'. Many small trays were also fitted with coloured glass bud vases, or were raised on pedestal bases, like cake stands. Although vast numbers were sold in the late 19th century, they are now quite scarce. As a result, they sell well, at £200-£300. Hopefully more and more examples will come on to the market, as the interest in plate spreads, but it seems very unlikely that prices will fall.

A Mappin Brothers of Sheffield 22in (55.9cm) gallery tea tray with attractive rim, pierced with paterae and swags. Made c.1880, this would sell for £500-£700. It is illustrated with an unmarked Art Deco coffee service with both hot milk jug and cream jug. Standard in design, and not stylishly Deco enough to be of great interest, this might cost as little as £150-£200.

An American late 19th century 21in (53.3cm) tray by Pairpoint of New Bedford, the ground engraved with a Japanese-style vignette of herons at a pool. Although badly worn, this is a handsome piece which might retail for £500-£700.

An American tray with cast mask handles and with an elaborate vacant strapwork cartouche. Made by Gorham of Providence, Rhode Island, c.1890, it measures a massive 33½in (85.1cm) long. It is, perhaps, too large to sell really well today. Nevertheless, it should realise £600-£800.

Above and left: *A rare and splendid American 'card receiver', no less than 39in (99.1cm) high, decorated with applied cast apple blossoms and fruit. The top is covered with spot-hammering, creating an attractive, sparkling effect. Made by The Meriden Britannia Co. in the 1880s, this piece is illustrated in their 1886-87 catalogue, priced at $70 with 'Old Silver' finish, 'Gold Inlay' adding on another $10. Today it would sell for £1,000-£1,200, if perfect.*

Card tables were also made by all the major American plate manufacturers. Highly ornate, these are now extremely difficult to find, as no doubt many were destroyed in the mid-20th century, when Victorian designs were much disliked. Today good examples retail for as much as £1,000-£1,200.

Tea and drinks trays were made in many different shapes, some standing on openwork scroll feet, and applied with gallery rims decorated with delicately pierced designs. Many late 19th century trays are so large and heavy that they are scarcely usable. Indeed, they often seem very unstable, as they feel as if they may buckle at any moment under their own weight. These huge, impractical examples are not popular today, retailing for £300-£500, although they do look most spectacular when standing on a sideboard. Smaller trays sell very well, however, often making £500-£700. They should retail for less if engraved with initials or a presentation inscription, unless, of course, this is of historical interest, mentioning a well-known character or event. Although inscriptions can be removed, it is an expensive operation, as the tray will then have to be replated. Moreover, the erasure of deep engraving will inevitably weaken the piece, as the silversmith may have to grind away a thick layer of metal before the inscription disappears altogether. It is far better to pay more for a plain tray, if you find inscriptions offensive. In fact, many collectors of plate do not seem to mind them, as they may be the only accurate way of dating an unmarked piece.

Alcoholic Objects

The whole range of tradional pieces such as goblets, labels and funnels continued to be manufactured, but the introduction of electroplate coincided with several new objects designed for the consumption of alcohol. The Tantalus, a lockable frame for two or more spirit decanters, was invented circa 1850. The majority had an oak frame with applied plated mounts, although examples made entirely in plate are not uncommon. Some more elaborate specimens incorporated cigar boxes and even games boxes, fitted with packs of playing cards, cribbage boards and chess sets. Named after the son of Zeus, who was condemned to stand up to his neck in water which receded every time he tried to drink, the Tantalus is still very popular, often selling for £500-£700 if complete and in good condition. You should avoid examples with broken or missing decanters, as it is very difficult to find replacements which fit into the frame.

Another introduction was the wine bottle holder, a hinged, folding frame which held a single bottle. Applied with a scroll handle, this was designed to facilitate pouring without the risk of spilling any of the contents. Still quite common, these useful pieces are inexpensive, at £100-£150.

Although one tends to think of cocktail sets and shakers as a 20th century invention, in fact they were introduced surprisingly early. Tiffany and Co.'s 1893

A magnificent trefoil decanter stand fitted with original green, red and mauve blown glass decanters gilt with trailing vines. The vine motif is repeated on the die-stamped neck mounts and cork finials as well as on the stand itself. 19in (48.3cm) high, this unmarked piece dates to c.1860. In perfect condition, it would sell for £700-£1,000. Empty stands are much cheaper, however, as it is very difficult to find decanters of the correct size.

The Tantalus was invented in the mid-19th century, as a means of preventing the servants from sampling the spirits locked away within the decanters. This unmarked 18in (45.7cm) example of c.1890 incorporates an added feature, a cedar-lined cigar box. Made of oak, with electroplated mounts, and still with its original and perfect cut-glass decanters, it would bring £700-£1,000. The labels are not original.

Blue Book, a catalogue of the company's wares, lists them for the first time. The vogue for cocktails soon reached Britain, enjoying its heyday in the 1920s and '30s. Huge numbers of accessories were manufactured, including measures, spoons and strainers. These became extremely popular a few years ago, when cocktails again became the fashionable drink. Today they are less saleable, and one can find inexpensive examples quite easily. Novelty specimens and stylishly Art Deco examples are still collected, however. Look out for revolving shakers engraved with recipes, or for curious shakers modelled as bells, dumb-bells, or animals. These can sell for several hundreds of pounds.

An 18in (45.7cm) wine trolley with cast rococo handle and machine-pierced coasters. Although the piece is unmarked, each of the coasters has a silver boss stamped with a lion passant and the Sheffield date letter for 1863. £400-£600.

An unmarked cut-glass sherry barrel with plated mounts and stand. 12in (30.5cm) long, this impressive piece would grace any sideboard, hence £600-£800. It is illustrated with an unmarked blown glass novelty wine jug fashioned as a dog, with plated collar and stopper. Crudely made, but still rather appealing, this would sell for £400-£500. Both pieces date from the late 19th century.

Two late 19th century bottle holders and a 6½in (16.5cm) wine funnel, each made by William Hutton and Sons of Sheffield c.1890. Although stamped 'E.P.', each is also impressed with the crossed arrows mark formerly used by T. and J. Creswick, manufacturers of fused plate (see page 220). Left to right: £120-£160, £40-£60, and £100-£120.

An American wine cooler designed to hold no fewer than two quart bottles and four pint bottles, the handles applied with cast soldiers in Civil War uniforms, the centre with a water nymph. The cover, with its pressed glass ice dishes, is detachable, so that the large bowl can be used for punch during the winter months. Manufactured by The Meriden Britannia Co. in the second half of the 19th century, this monumental piece is 26½in (67.3cm) high. It warrants a full-page illustration in the 1886-87 catalogue, where it is priced at a staggering $275. Today it might cost £2,500-£3,500.

Finally, splendid iced water and lemonade pitchers, usually made of plated Britannia metal, first appeared in the last quarter of the 19th century. Large and imposing, they were often sold as part of a set with a pair of goblets and a waste bowl. Some are so large that, when full, one can hardly lift them. Recognising this drawback, the manufacturers thoughtfully provided stands upon which the pitchers balanced, tipping forwards when one wished to serve a drink. Commonly known as 'tilters', these magnificent objects are now very popular, retailing for at least £700-£1,000 if complete. Smaller versions were also made in America, used to serve maple syrup at breakfast time.

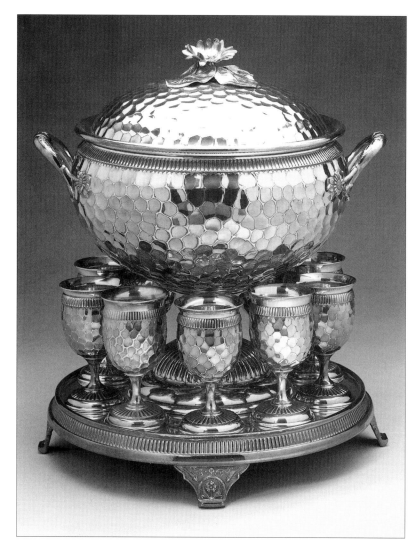

Perhaps made more for presentation than actually for imbibing, this 12in (30.5cm) goblet is engraved with a horse and sulky. The racing theme is continued on the stem, applied with a jockey's cap, a whip, and the winner's laurel wreath. Manufactured by Pairpoint of New Bedford, Massachusetts, c.1880, it would now realise £300-£400, probably selling to a collector of racing memorabilia rather than to a collector of plate.

An American late 19th century 16in (40.6cm) punch bowl and stand with twelve cups, each piece decorated with a sparkling spot-hammered finish. Made by Reed and Barton of Taunton, Massachusetts, it would sell for £800-£1,200.

An unusual American 5½in (14cm) Britannia metal spirit flask die-stamped with an elaborate floral design, the cap applied with a collapsible nickel silver tot cup. Made by Simpson, Hall, Miller and Co. of Wallingford, Connecticut, c.1870, it should cost no more than £100-£150. (See Marks, page 220.)

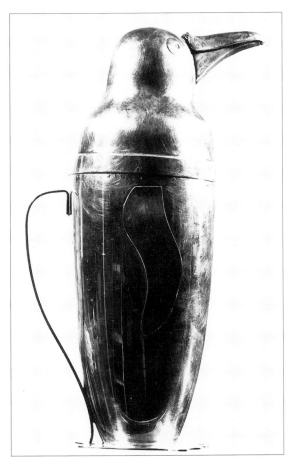

1920s and 1930s cocktail shakers are still very common. After experiencing a boom in popularity some five years ago they are now less saleable, plain examples retailing for as little as £30-£50. Novelty specimens are still collected, however, and this unmarked 12in (30.5cm) 'penguin' shaker should bring at least £200-£300.

Above right: One of the more impressive pieces of American plate, the iced water pitcher, commonly known as a 'tilter', was a popular wedding gift during the last quarter of the 19th century. This 20½in (52.1cm) example, by The Meriden Britannia Co., still has its original goblets and waste bowl, hence £700-£1,000.

An American late 19th century 15in (38.1cm) water pitcher in the Japanese taste, decorated with spot-hammered facets and applied with gilt flowers and a dragonfly. Manufactured by The Meriden Britannia Co. c.1880, this would sell for £300-£500.

A splendid unmarked 16½in (41.9cm) oak water pitcher with nickel foot mount and cover. The other details are made from copper, the plaques, depicting spirited battle scenes, formed by electrotyping. This piece, tremendously heavy as it has a thick pottery liner to insulate the contents, is applied with an extra handle at the front. Without this it would be difficult to lift the pitcher, let alone pour out its contents. Typical of the so-called 'Medieval' style, extremely popular in the mid-19th century, it would now retail for £600-£800.

Writing Equipment

Although the makers of electroplate produced a large number of inkstands and wells in traditional designs, they also made made a vast range of novelty pieces, taking full advantage of the fact that cast base metal could now be plated with great success. Animal and bird designs were especially popular with the sentimental Victorians, both in Britain and in America. Realistically modelled, these have returned to favour after many years of neglect, now selling extremely well.

Other desk accessories, such as paper knives and weights, blotters, pen wipes and stamp boxes, were also made in plate, many again applied with tiny but detailed cast figures, both human and animal. The 19th century desk was also covered with a host of other knick-knacks such as photograph frames, bells, clocks, rulers and perpetual calendars, perhaps the Victorian equivalents of the modern 'executive toys'. Indeed, Queen Victoria's writing table at Windsor was so cluttered with bric-a-brac, it was said to 'resemble a stall at a fancy bazaar'. One wonders how our ancestors managed to find enough room to actually write their correspondence! Despite the introduction of the telephone, leading to the general decline of personal letter-writing, 19th and early 20th century desk plate is much prized. It has become fashionable for modern businessmen to personalise their streamlined offices by decorating them with antique writing equipment, so prices have risen dramatically over the last decade.

Novelty inkstands are perennial favourites with the modern collector. Here we see a splendid American example by The Meriden Britannia Co., modelled with two cats' heads applied with realistic green glass eyes. 8½in (21.6cm) long, it dates from c.1880. £400-£600. Notice that it has an almost identical die-rolled border to the teaset illustrated at the bottom of page 178. Obviously, frugal manufacturers standardised their mounts as much as possible in order to ecnomise.

197

This 6½in (16.5cm) inkwell is cast in Britannia metal, the soft alloy reproducing the tasselled headdress and even the texture of the elephant's skin in great detail. Manufactured by The Meriden Britannia Co. c.1875, it would now bring £300-£500. In the 1886-87 catalogue it is priced at $6.

A splendid plated nickel inkstand with hobnail pattern cut-glass inkwells. The cast Britannia metal ram's head opens to reveal a wafer box or stamp container. Unmarked, this 12½in (31.8cm) piece was made c.1870. £600-£800.

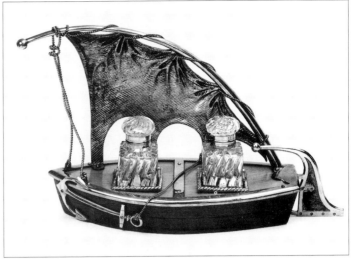

An unmarked 12½in (31.8cm) plate and oak boat inkstand with moulded glass wells, the sail cast in Britannia metal, the other mounts made of nickel. Manufactured c.1890, this would sell for £300-£400.

Left: An unmarked cast spelter 7½in (19.1cm) bird inkwell opening to reveal a pottery well. Although the outside has been cleaned right down to the base metal, one can see that the interior of the head is still bright with electroplating. This piece is probably British, dating to c.1890. £150-£200.

A 6in (15.2cm) horse's hoof inkstand with stamp box and crossed riding crop pen rest. Although unmarked, it can be dated accurately as the front is applied with a plaque engraved, rather poignantly: 'In Memory of Kitty, Dad's Pal, August 25, 1911'. £200-£250.

An Elkington and Co. 8in (20.3cm) electrotyped inkwell decorated with classical figures, griffins and flowers. Examples of this mass-produced inkwell were produced throughout the second half of the 19th century, and are still quite common, hence £180-£220.

A splendid 19in (48.3cm) inkstand on an oak base, the dolphins' bodies fashioned from rams' horns, their heads and tails cast in Britannia metal. Remarkably complete, it still has its original inkwells plus a clock and a bell to summon the servants. Unmarked and made c.1870, this would sell for £600-£800.

A rare mid-19th century electrotyped portable desk with writing slope, inkwells and a taperstick. Unmarked, this attractive piece could sell for £1,000-£1,500.

This charming piece, made by Joseph Rodgers and Sons of Sheffield in the late 19th century, has an ivory base and body with applied electroplate mounts. The 4¾in (12.1cm) pot, possibly designed to hold an inkwell, is supported by two cast blackamoors straining to carry their load. £300-£400.

An Art Nouveau electrotyped desk blotter decorated with four rural vignettes surrounded by stylised pine cones. The cartouche in the centre is moulded with mistletoe, a plant much used by turn-of-the-century designers. Unmarked, this 12½in (31.8cm) piece would retail for £200-£300.

A splendid electrotyped double photograph frame decorated with well-modelled putti and an angel. Although unmarked, one could pay as much as £300-£400 for this 13in (33cm) piece, as it is both practical and very impressive.

Miscellaneous Pieces

Almost every room in the over-furnished Victorian home was cluttered with electroplated pieces, some functional, others purely decorative. A large range of objects were fashioned for bedroom use, and the dressing table was covered with a collection of pots and bottles, trinket boxes and jewellery cases, pin cushions, hair tidies, brushes, combs and mirrors. Many were extremely ornate, with sparkling spot-hammered finishes, or with matt surfaces enlivened with Japanese-style engraved decoration enhanced with gilding. Other 'dresser sets', particularly popular in America, were fitted with cut or coloured glass bottles, the latter enamelled with Kate Greenaway style figures, butterflies and flowers. All are now much collected, as are smaller, more personal pieces of electroplate such as chatelaines, perfume bottles and vinaigrettes. These bibelots were seen purely as 'dust-collectors' or worthless bric-a-brac until recently, but now there is a great demand for them, and they retail

Two more American bedroom pieces, a 6½in (16.5cm) basket-form trinket box by Simpson, Hall, Miller and Co. of Wallingford, and a combination jewellery box and pin cushion by Reed and Barton of Taunton, almost 11in (27.9cm) high. The latter operates in the same way as the previous piece. Both were made c.1880, and would sell for £100-£150 and £200-£300 respectively.

Made, I suspect, more for show than for use, this unmarked plated nickel ewer and basin are decorated with attractive narrow flutes and applied cast gadrooning. In fact they are rather impractical, as the foot of the ewer is too small to support the heavy body securely. Manufactured in the late 19th or early 20th century, they would now sell for £400-£500.

An American dressing-table mirror hammered with a honeycomb effect of hexagons and applied with a cast cherub and with gilt flowers, a bird and a butterfly. Manufactured by The Meriden Britannia Co. c.1875, this 22½in (57.2cm) piece would now be immensely popular, retailing for at least £600-£800.

This massive electroplated ewer, 15¾in (40cm) high, inset with numerous facsimile coins, is a late 19th century adaptation of the 17th century style. Although impressive at first glance, it is of poor quality, the feet cast in Britannia metal, a soft lead alloy very prone to damage. £300-£400.

An unusual jewellery box fashioned from an emu egg with unmarked electroplated mounts and mirrored lid. Applied with the name of the original owner and dating to the late 19th century, this rare piece, 6¾in (17.1cm) wide, may have been made in Australia. £300-£400.

A set of six unmarked electroplate novelty menu-holders modelled as swans, probably dating to the late 19th century, each 2in (5.1cm) high. While the case is a little shabby, the pieces themselves are in perfect condition. Although these items may have been made in Britain, the tooled decoration on their leather case would suggest manufacture in France. £400-£600.

A marvellous Victorian unmarked 15in (38.1cm) revolving sewing stand of c.1870, fitted with numerous reels of cotton and thimbles, and with a central pin cushion. Difficult to use, as it has an extremely fragile blown glass dome, it may have been manufactured as a display piece for a millinery shop window. I am not sure whether the cast figures of dancing Irishmen, each clutching a shillelagh, have any significance. I suspect the maker of this piece simply took two figures at random from the stockroom. These would actually have been made as finials for trophy cups. £800-£1,200.

A great number of smokers' requisites were manufactured in electroplate throughout the second half of the 19th century. All are now avidly collected. This parcel-gilt 4½in (11.4cm) combination cigar holder and tobacco jar is an electrotype, manufactured by Elkington and Co. in 1877. (See Marks, page 220.) Decorated with a charming frieze of dancing putti, it is reproduced in fine detail. Unfortunately it should have a lid for the tobacco jar. As this is missing, the piece should cost no more than £100-£150. A complete specimen would retail for £300-£400.

for astonishing prices. There is also a strong market for sewing accessories of all kinds, and plated advertising thimbles, stamped with the names of various products ranging from perfumes and patent medicines to horse linament, can bring as much as £30-£50 each.

Smoking requisites are also very popular with the modern buyer, despite the current disfavour the tobacco industry is receiving. Small pieces such as snuff boxes make ideal pill boxes, while vesta cases, known as match safes in America, are worn as unusual pendants or displayed on coffee tables. Cigar boxes or humidors, and tobacco jars sell well too, as do novelty cigar lighters and match holders, often modelled in the shapes of various animals and birds.

One can go through the catalogues of prolific 19th century manufacturers to find many other examples of electroplate, now scarce and expensive. A peculiarly American creation was the fireman's trumpet, awarded for great acts of courage. The Meriden Britannia Co.'s catalogue of 1886-87 has a choice of five designs, each engraved with a fire tender or with other symbols of the profession. The most expensive, 'Nickel Silver, Silver Soldered, Repousse and Engraved, Silver and Gold Inlaid', cost an enormous $150, although one could buy a simpler, smaller trumpet for $16.75. In both cases, 'cord and tassels' added $3.25 to the price.

Children's christening mugs were also made in many different designs, ranging in price from $1 for a pretty example delicately-engraved with a humming-bird. There is, however, a footnote, warning that this piece is made of 'single plate', and does not bear the trade mark of the company. Obviously, it was bought in from elsewhere, to

A 7in (17.8cm) tobacco jar and ashtray, the lid applied with a match holder. This piece, made from plated nickel c.1880, has an impressed maker's mark, 'J. Y. and S.', so far untraced. One side is engraved with putto musicians, the other with Shakespeare's Falstaff, a 'church warden' pipe in his hand. £200-£250.

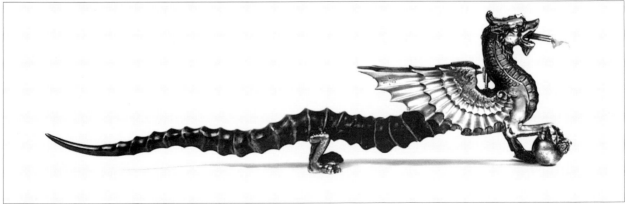

The 'Dragon' cigar lighter by Walker and Hall of Sheffield, with electroplated Britannia metal mounts applied to a blackbuck horn, the latter ideal for suggesting the body of the mythical beast. This splendid 16in (40.6cm) object, 'Especially suitable for Clubs, Regimental and Naval Messes, etc.', is illustrated in an undated manufacturers' catalogue, priced at £5 15s 6d. Today it would bring £300-£500. This design was made from the late 19th century until the 1930s.

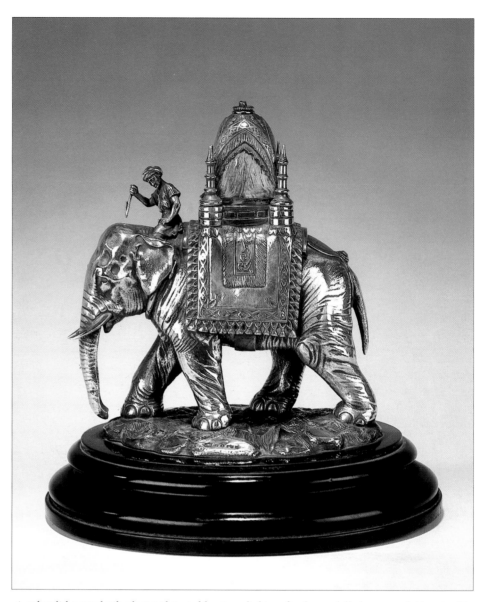

A splendid parcel-gilt electroplate table cigar-lighter, finely modelled as an elephant with mahout and howdah, the latter containing the fuel. The top of this piece would have held a lighted wick used to ignite four smaller wicks held by the four gilt pillars at each corner of the howdah. Victorian novelty pieces are currently in great demand, and I would expect this 9in (22.9cm) piece to sell for at least £600-800.

satisfy the demand for a cheap, but nonetheless attractive, little cup. Boxed christening sets with mugs, cutlery and napkin rings were also provided, while the adult might receive as a gift a moustache cup or a shaving mug, some fitted with detachable soap boxes, or a card case or purse. It is worth remembering that these curios were not restricted to the 19th century. An undated Walker and Hall catalogue, probably printed in the 1930s, illustrates several oddities including razor strops, 'shingled hair sets', 'houbigant cases', presentation keys and 'launching scissors', given to the celebrity who opened a new building, and trowels and mallets used to lay foundation stones, as well as some splendid 'surprise tables' mounted on castors. These were fitted with teasets or 'liquor' sets which disappeared from view 'when the table leaves are raised and folded', converting the cabinet into a table which could then be wheeled from the drawing room. All of these strange objects would sell well today, as there is a strong and steady demand for unusual electroplate.

A reproduction electroplated salver 14½in (36.8cm) in diameter. The design of this piece is closely based on those of the mid-18th century and, combined with the red glow of copper in the worn centre, perhaps might lead the unwary buyer to think it is made of Old Sheffield plate. In fact, the piece is clearly marked: 'Primrose Plate' and 'EP Copper', along with the tell-tale 'Made in England', the latter denoting manufacture no earlier than the 1920s. This particular salver was probably made within the last thirty years. £50-£80.

An unmarked novelty 5½in (14cm) cigar lighter on rockwork base. The detachable handle of the frog's cane contains a small wick which one lights from the 'cigar' in the creature's mouth This small piece, made c.1890, would be very popular today, retailing for £200-£300.

An American naturalistic smoker's stand with three various 'tree stump' containers for cigars, cigarettes and matches, one applied with an axe. Manufactured by Pairpoint of New Bedford c.1890, this appealing piece would sell for £300-£400. It is 9in (22.9cm) wide.

Three vesta cases, all made from electroplated base metal. Inexpensive novelties when first sold, they are now much collected. Left to right: A 2in (5.1cm) boot with suspension loop, £70-£100; an oblong example applied with a plastic railway ticket, £100-£150; the bust of Prime Minister Gladstone, £100-£150. All date from the second half of the 19th century.

The Care of Electroplate

The section on the care of Old Sheffield plate should be read, as the cleaning methods and prevention of tarnish apply equally to electroplate. Cleaning may have to be tackled more often, as electroplated pieces are covered with pure silver rather than with sterling silver. Pure silver tarnishes more quickly when exposed to the atmosphere, so it is better to display your collection behind glass where possible.

The great advantage of electroplate over fused plate is that it can be replated when worn. This does no harm whatsoever, as it merely repeats the initial process of decoration. As Dorothy T. and H. Ivan Rainwater remark, in *American Silverplate*, 'A few dealers and collectors have been heard to remark that they would not have old silverplated pieces replated because it would destroy their value as antiques. This is utter nonsense. Electroplating "Old Sheffield Plate" would lower its value, it is true, as the original process of plating was entirely different. Replating old electro-

A complete late 19th century Holy Communion set by Henry Wilkinson and Co. of Sheffield, its plain design reproducing the style of the early to mid-18th century. Church plate is difficult to sell, although one could use the 11½in (29.2 cm) flagon as a claret jug, and the paten as a dessert stand. £250-£300.

A marvellous late 19th century Britannia metal jardinière modelled as a long-eared owl, with realistic bright orange glass eyes. Cast in two sections, each side depicts the same striking design. Unmarked, this large piece, almost 12in (30.5cm) in diameter, might retail for as much as £800-£1,200, even though it is somewhat worn.

An electroplated cakestand, the body made from copper, the cast and applied border from Britannia metal. This material is ideal for casting as it can be moulded with fine details. Made within the last thirty years, this 7in (17.8cm) piece is clearly marked 'Old English Reproduction, EP on Copper, BM Mounted'. £60-£80.

silverplate, though, is simply to restore it to its original condition.' If you send worn pieces for replating they must first be chemically stripped, to remove traces of remaining plate as well as oxides which have formed on the surface. This ensures that the new deposits of silver will adhere firmly. Once thoroughly cleaned, repairs are carried out, and then the piece is cleaned once again. It is now ready to be 'dipped' into the plating vat. After buffing and polishing it will be returned, as good as new. The only problem with replating is that it works so perfectly. Your pieces may seem too bright and clean. You may rest assured that they will soon tarnish once again, regaining the colour and the dullness of old electroplate.

This modern Regency style 10in (25.4cm) salver has an applied gadroon and shell border and a pierced gallery. Although the ground appears to be hand-chased, the frieze of arabesques surrounding the cartouche is actually machine stamped, and closer examination of the piece soon reveals that it is actually of rather poor quality, the border lacking detail and with an ugly granular finish. £40-£60.

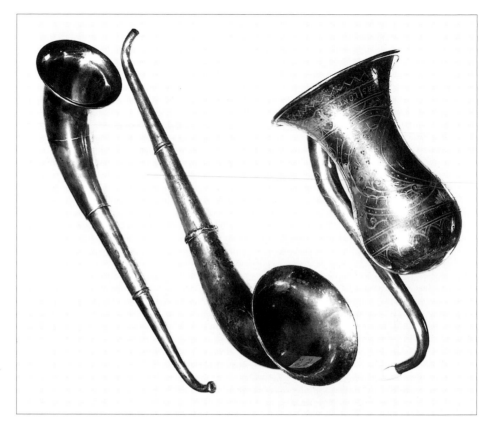

Medical curiosities sell very well, as they are avidly collected by modern doctors. Here we see a selection of three ear trumpets, the two plain examples c.1860. The engraved bulbous 10in (25.4cm) trumpet was made a little later, probably dating from the last quarter of the 19th century. All are unmarked. £400-£600 each.

Marks on Plate

The buyer of British silver has been protected for centuries by the stamping of hallmarks, a regular set of punches showing quality of silver and date of manufacture as well as the maker and the town where each piece was assayed. Continental and American silver is also usually clearly marked, although here the punches are often less easy to decipher.

Collectors of plate may find a wide array of marks, but they are also, on the other hand, often faced with a wealth of unmarked material, which they have to evaluate by quality, and date by style. T. W. Frost sums up this problem in his book, *The Price Guide to Old Sheffield Plate*, when he writes: 'Finally, too much emphasis should not be put on the presence or absence of marks on articles of Old Sheffield plate. After all it is the quality of the piece which is ultimately of greatest importance'. His remarks apply equally well to all forms of plating, although one should point out that, given a choice between two similar objects, one marked, the other unmarked, then the collector should always buy the marked example.

When marks do appear on plate they are often difficult to trace. A great number can now be found in reference books, the American companies being particularly well covered in recent works, but there are even more marks, the origins of which have not yet been discovered. One assumes that, as plate becomes more and more collected, scholars will take the time and trouble to carry out more extensive research, hopefully coming up with answers to fill the gaps in our knowledge.

This book makes no attempt to list and describe the range of makers' marks which one may find. However, I include some illustrations of the marks seen on some of the items pictured in the text, to give the reader an idea of what to look out for. Marks can be divided into several categories, as follows:

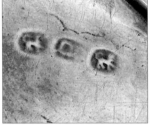

Page 12: *A salver worn from years of cleaning, the marks were devised to deceive. Notice the attempts to copy the lion passant stamp of sterling silver. The other punch is presumably meant to be a date letter or maker's mark.*

Page 18: *A typical close plate mark, the maker's surname in full, along with a trade mark symbol. Notice the bubbling of the silver, caused by damp.*

Page 29: *A curious, unidentified punch which can often be found on early items of Old Sheffield plate, dating from the 1760s.*

Makers' marks

In the early days of plate these were made to look as much like silver hallmarks as possible. Silversmiths feared the loss of their trade, and managed to petition Parliament which, in 1773, banned the striking of marks on pieces 'made of metal, plated or covered with silver, or upon any metal vessel or other thing made to look like silver'. This law was repealed in 1784, and now plate-makers were allowed to strike their wares with their surnames plus any 'mark, figure or device' they might choose. This could not clash with silver, as silversmiths were now using their initials to mark their output.

Electroplate frequently bears makers' initials, along with other marks meant to resemble silver hallmarks. Many pieces were stamped with a crown, the assay mark of the city of Sheffield, while others were struck with curious animals, obviously copying the lion passant of sterling silver. The makers of hallmarked silver were, justifiably, very concerned about this. Although they were once again successful in petitioning Parliament, there were many infringements of the law.

Workmen's Marks

The workers of the plate industry were often paid on a pro rata basis, the foreman counting up their output each day so that they could be fairly rewarded at the end of the week. The foreman also had to be able to distinguish between each of his workers' wares, so that poor workmanship could be traced back to its source. Thus a system was devised, in larger companies, where each member of staff had his own punch, sometimes cut with initials, but more often cut with a small symbol such as a star or a leaf. These were usually stamped on to hidden places of each article, such as inside a candlestick nozzle.

Retailers' marks

Much plate was unmarked by the factory, as important retailers preferred to use their own punches, thus implying that they had actually manufactured their wares, rather than simply bought them in for resale. Retailers' marks usually give a name in full, as well as their address.

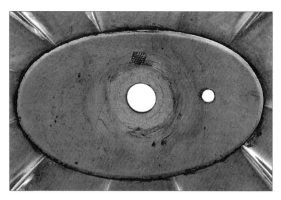

Page 65, bottom left: *A quality mark, designed to impress potential customers. In fact, I doubt whether this piece is any better than other Old Sheffield plate of the period, the first quarter of the 19th century. Notice that the interior of this piece is tinned.*

Page 65, bottom right: *A very common fused plate maker's mark, the crossed arrows of T. and J. Creswick. It was later used to mark electroplate, as we shall see. Once again, the interior of this piece is tinned.*

Page 95, bottom: *The mark of I. and I. Waterhouse and Co., their initials with a fleur-de-lis. Notice the overturned silver rim on this salver.*

Page 101, top: *Surely the most familiar mark of all, the double sunburst used by Matthew Boulton, of Birmingham. Its presence will add at least 50% to the asking price.*

Stock Numbers

The major manufacturers of plate produced well-illustrated catalogues, providing each item in their range with a stock number, so that retailers could reorder without any confusion. These numbers, often with four figures, were stamped or engraved on to each piece. All too often, the amateur assumes these are dates, endowing his finds with a totally fictitious history.

Quality Marks

Many companies made items with varying thicknesses of silver plating, the customer paying more for extra silver as this meant, in theory if not always in practice, that his purchases would have a longer life. Some firms marked their better wares with an 'A1' punch, while others came up with trade names such as 'Mappin and Webb Prince's Plate', or 'Adelphi quadruple plate'.

Date marks

Most plate cannot be dated with accuracy, although Elkington and Co. did use a series of date letters starting in 1841, maintaining their system until as recently as 1986. Many 19th century British pieces are impressed with a diamond registration mark, and one can work out the date when a design was registered at the Patent

Page 115, left: *An impressed mark which can often be seen on cups and tankards. The crudely-scratched numbers are probably those of pawn-brokers, who often marked their pledges in this way.*

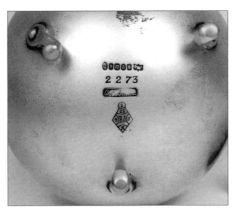

Page 137, top: *A very full set of marks, reading, top to bottom, left to right: 'E.P.', a descriptive mark showing that the piece is made of electroplate. There then follow the makers' initials for James Dixon and Sons, along with their trade mark, a bugle. We then see a stock number, followed by the all important impressed signature of Dr. Christopher Dresser. Finally, a diamond registration mark for 1880.*

Page 142, bottom: *An engraved mark, dating from the early days of electroplating. Perhaps Mary Fox visited the Elkingtons' laboratory, and was then given this bowl as a souvenir.*

Page 155: *Another comprehensive series of marks showing the makers along with their trade mark, implying extra thickness of silver plating. This is followed by a patent registration number and a stock number.*

Page 158: *Here we see a typically detailed Tiffany and Co. mark, which even gives the size of the platter upon which it is stamped. Notice the word 'Double', implying a greater thickness of plating.*

Page 162, bottom: *Henry Wilkinson and Co.'s initials with their trade mark, two crossed keys, followed by a stock number. The initials 'T.H.' are those of the workman who actually made the piece.*

Office quite easily. One must remember however, that popular designs might have been made for many years after patent registration. This is also the case for American pieces, often impressed with a patent date.

Descriptive Marks

These are usually very straightforward sets of initials such as: 'E.P.N.S.', for electroplated nickel silver, or: 'E.P.B.M.', for electroplated Britannia metal. Some makers went to great lengths to disguise their plated wares however, without actually telling lies. Thus, Tiffany and Co. stamped much of their plate 'Silver-soldered'. This euphemism meant little to the average buyer, although those in the know were aware that this mark was not used on sterling silver wares.

Page 164, top: *Makers' surnames Mappin and Webb impressed in full, with a stock number and a diamond registration mark for 1867.*

Page 165, bottom: *Although this basket is clearly marked 'E.P.', the arrangement of the marks and the use of the Sheffield crown would suggest that a certain amount of deception is taking place. At a glance one would certainly think that this piece is made of sterling silver. The impressed 'A' presumably suggests that the item is of 'A1', or top, quality.*

Page 168, top: *Another piece by James Dixon and Sons. Notice the stamped legend, '90 oz', used to suggest that more silver was plated on to this biscuit warmer, by leaving it for a longer period in the plating vat.*

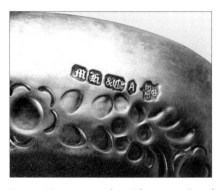

Page 173, top right: *The initials of Martin Hall and Co. of Sheffield, along with a quality mark and a descriptive mark. Once again, the crown is used in a rather misleading way.*

Page 176, top: *One of the many marks used by The Meriden Britannia Co., explaining why American collectors invariably familiarly refer to the company as 'Meriden B'. We also see a quality mark and a stock number.*

Page 180, top: *A maker's name in full, with a stock number and a quality mark. This arrangement is typical for British electroplated Britannia metal.*

Miscellaneous Marks

Many trade terms were used deliberately to confuse the buyer, who could be misled into thinking he had purchased sterling silver at bargain prices. I recently examined a batch of flatware delivered to Christie's for eventual auction, noting the following: 'Argentine Silver', 'Brazilian Silver', and 'Imperial Silver'. All were made of electroplate! There are many other similarly confusing terms, and one should never accept a mark at face value.

Page 192, bottom: *Crossed arrows used by William Hutton and Sons, along with the company's initials, a quality mark, 'Hard soldered', and a stock number. The initials in the trefoil punch are those of the metalworker who made this piece.*

A variation of William Hutton and Sons' mark, with a different quality mark, 'A.1.' and, of course, a different stock number.

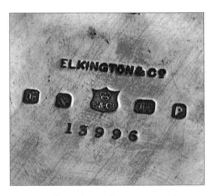

Page 194, bottom: *It is not surprising that this mark is similar to that of The Meriden Britannia Co. Both firms eventually became part of The International Silver Co., a huge conglomerate founded in 1898 in 'Silver City', Meriden, Connecticut.*

Page 206, right: *Elkington and Co.'s mark, with their date letter for 1877. Their name is also given in full, along with a stock number.*

Marks on Old Sheffield Plate

John Allgood,
Birmingham
June 1812

Ashforth & Co.,
Sheffield
Oct. 1784

Ashley,
Birmingham
Dec. 1816

Willm. Banister,
Birmingham
Mar. 1808

Barnet
1808

Beldon, Hoyland &
Co., Sheffield
Aug. 1785

Geo. Beldon,
Sheffield
May 1809

Henry Best,
Birmingham
Dec. 1814

Best & Wastidge,
Sheffield
Oct. 1816

William Bingley,
Birmingham
Oct. 1787

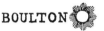

Boulton,
Birmingham
Oct. 1784

Joseph Bradshaw,
Birmingham
Feb. 1822

Brittain, Wilkinson &
Brownill, Sheffield
July 1785

T. Butts,
Birmingham
Aug.1807

Thomas Cheston,
Birmingham
Mar. 1809

Thomas Child,
Birmingham
June 1821

Willm. Coldwell,
Sheffield
April 1806

James Corn & Jno.
Sheppard,
Birmingham
July 1819

John Cracknall,
Birmingham
Mar. 1814

Thos. & James
Creswick, Sheffield
July 1811

John Davis,
Birmingham
Oct. 1816

Deakin, Smith &
Co., Sheffield
July 1785

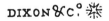

Dixon & Co.,
Birmingham
Sept. 1784

James Dixon &
Son, Sheffield
July 1835

George Bott Dunn,
Birmingham
Oct. 1810

Saml. Evans,
Birmingham
Dec. 1816

John Fletcher Causer,
Birmingham
April 1824

Fox, Proctor,
Pasmore & Co.,
Sheffield
Sept. 1784

Henry Froeth,
Birmingham
May 1816

Froggatt, Coldwell &
Co., Sheffield
1797

Robt. Gainsford,
Sheffield
July 1808

William Garnett,
Sheffield
July 1803

Josh. Gibbs,
Birmingham
Feb. 1807

John Gilbert,
Birmingham
Mar. 1812

Alexr. Goodman &
Co., Sheffield
July 1800

Edward Goodwin,
Sheffield
July 1794

John Green & Co.,
Sheffield
Jan. 1799

Joseph Green,
Birmingham
April 1807

W. Green & Co.,
Sheffield
Sept. 1784

Charles Gretter
Cope, Birmingham
July 1817

   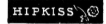

Willm. Hall,
Birmingham
April 1820

Mats. Hanson,
Birmingham
April 1810

Joseph Harrison,
Birmingham
Aug. 1809

Aaron Hatfield,
Sheffield
Mar. 1808

Aaron Hatfield,
Sheffield
April 1810

Daniel Hill & Co.,
Birmingham
Dec. 1806

Josh Hinks,
Birmingham
Oct. 1812

J. Hipkiss,
Birmingham
Feb. 1808

Wm Hipwood,
Birmingham
Nov. 1809

Holland & Co.,
Birmingham
Sept. 1784

David Horton,
Birmingham
Jan. 1808

Jno. Horton,
Birmingham
April 1809

Stanley & Thos.
Howard, London
May 1809

Wm. Hutton,
Birmingham
Nov. 1807

William Jarvis,
Sheffield
Feb. 1789

James Johnson,
Birmingham
Mar. 1812

Jones, Birmingham
June 1824

Thomas Jordan,
Birmingham
July 1814

Samuel Kirkby,
Sheffield
Jan. 1812

John Law,
Sheffield
Jan. 1810

John Law & Son,
Sheffield
Jan. 1807

Richd. Law,
Birmingham
Nov. 1807

Thos. Law & Co.,
Sheffield
Sept. 1784

Abner Cowel Lea,
Birmingham
Dec. 1808

George Lees,
Birmingham
Feb. 1810

Joseph Lilly,
Birmingham
Oct. 1816

LINWOOD
John Linwood,
Birmingham
April 1807

John Linwood,
Birmingham
Nov. 1807

Mathw. Linwood &
Son, Birmingham
July 1808

Willm. Linwood,
Birmingham
Nov. 1807

Love, Silverside,
Darby & Co., Sheffield
June 1785

John Love & Co.,
Sheffield
Mar. 1785

John Lylly,
Birmingham
Oct. 1815

P. Madin & Co.,
Sheffield
April 1788

Willm. Markland,
Birmingham
Mar. 1818

Heny. Meredith,
Birmingham
Dec. 1807

Moore,
Birmingham
Sept. 1784

Fredrick Moore,
Birmingham
Mar. 1820

Richard Morton &
Co., Sheffield
Mar. 1785

William Newbould
& Sons, Sheffield
Oct. 1804

Jas. Nicholds,
Birmingham
Mar. 1808

Danl. Holy Parker &
Co., Sheffield
Oct. 1804

John Parsons & Co.,
Sheffield
Sept. 1784

Peake,
Birmingham
July 1807

Richard Pearson,
Birmingham
Dec. 1811

Richard Pearson,
Birmingham
July 1813

Pemberton & Mitchell,
Birmingham
Nov. 1817

Saml. Pimley,
Birmingham
April 1810

ROBERTS
& CADMAN
Roberts & Cadman,
Sheffield
July 1785

I & S.
ROBERTS.
Samuel Roberts &
Co., Sheffield
May 1786

ROD
GERS
Joseph Rodgers &
Son, Sheffield
July 1822

ROGERS
Jno. Rogers,
Birmingham
April 1819

Willm. Ryland &
Sons, Birmingham
Feb. 1807

Willm. Ryland &
Sons, Birmingham
Feb. 1807

Thos Sansom &
Sons, Sheffield
Oct. 1821

Wm. Scot,
Birmingham
Dec. 1807

Joseph Shephard,
Birmingham
April 1817

Robert Silk,
Birmingham
April 1809

Willm. Silkirk,
Birmingham
Sept. 1807

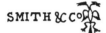
Thos Small,
Birmingham
June 1812

Smith & Co.,
Birmingham
Sept. 1784

George Smith, Tate,
Willm. Nicholson
and Hoult, Sheffield
Oct. 1810

Isaac Smith,
Birmingham
Jan. 1821

N. Smith & Co.,
Sheffield
Sept. 1784

Willm. Smith,
Birmingham
Feb. 1812

Staniforth, Parkin &
Co., Sheffield
Sept. 1784

Benjn. Stot, Sheffield
Feb. 1811

Robert Sutcliff & Co.,
Sheffield
Jan. 1786

Sykes & Co., Sheffield
Sept. 1784

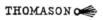
Stephen Thomas,
Birmingham
Feb. 1813

Edwd. Thomasons &
Dowler, Birmingham
Feb. 1807

Edwd. Thomasons &
Dowler, Birmingham
Mar. 1807

Tonks, Birmingham
Aug. 1807

Tonks, Birmingham
June 1824

Tudor & Co.,
Sheffield
Sept. 1784

Saml. Turley,
Birmingham
Dec. 1816

John Turton,
Birmingham
Sept. 1820

Joseph Tyndall,
Birmingham
July 1813

Waterhouse & Co.,
Birmingham
April 1807

I. & I. Waterhouse &
Co., Sheffield
Feb. 1833

John Waterhouse
Edward Hatfield & Co.,
Sheffield June 1836

Watson, Fenton &
Bradbury, Sheffield
Oct. 1795

Watson, Pass & Co.,
Sheffield
April 1811

John White,
Birmingham
Sept. 1811

Danl. Holy,
Wilkinson & Co.,
Sheffield
Sept. 1784

Henry Wilkinson &
Co., Sheffield
Jan. 1836

Robert Frederick
Wilkinson, James
Drabble, Henry
Mylins, Robert
Robinson, George
Battie, Alexander
Goodwin Turner,
Sheffield
Jan. 1805

Joseph Willmore,
Birmingham
Aug. 1807

Willm. Woodward,
Birmingham
July 1814

Sam Worton,
Birmingham
Jan. 1821

Jno. Wright & Geo.
Fairbairn, Sheffield
Mar. 1809

S. & C. Young & Co.,
Sheffield
July 1813

Marks on Electroplate

Early Elkington electroplate was marked with 'E & Co.', crowned in a shield and with the word ELEC TRO PLATE divided into three.

1840

1841

In 1841, then in 1842, the mark was changed and a date number added.

1842-64

1865-97

This series of numbers ran from 1 to 8 (with the 6 reversed). In 1849 letters were used, beginning with K. In 1865 the new series of letters started and the mark was also changed. B, C, I and J were omitted and Q was used as well as R in 1877. Slightly different marks were used from 1898-99 and from 1900 onwards.

1849-64

1865-85

1886-1911

1898-99

1900 onwards

The series beginning in 1912 omitted Q and that beginning in 1937 missed C and Q.

1912-36

1937-60

1961-86

225

Glossary

ACANTHUS: A plant with broad, scalloped leaves, the latter first used, in a stylised form, as a decorative motif by the Greeks.

AESTHETIC STYLE: A fashion introduced from Japan in the 1870s, and soon popular both in Britain and America. It was characterised by bright-cut birds, insects, and plants, frosting, and curious fan-shapes.

AMALGAM: An alloy of two or more metals, one of them often mercury.

AMORINO: A little cherub, also known as a putto, often used to enliven silver in the rococo period and by the Victorians.

ARABESQUES: An intricate woven design of scrolling foliage and flowers.

ARMORIAL: A family coat-of-arms, sometimes incorporating a crest.

ASSAY: To test a silver alloy, to verify that it comes up to the required standard.

BAKELITE: A type of rigid plastic invented in the 19th century.

BALUSTER: A slender pear-shape, used for such items as finials, candlestick stems, and knife handles.

BATWING FLUTING: A series of tapering vertical flutes which resemble an upside-down umbrella.

BEADING: An ornamental edging made from tiny half spheres or beads, particularly popular in the late 18th century, when it was commonly known as PEARLING.

BRIGHT-CUT: A technique of engraving using a special tool to create polished facets. These catch the light to give an attractive, sparkling effect.

BRITANNIA METAL: A silvery-white alloy of tin hardened with antimony and copper.

BUFFING: The polishing of silver, usually by machine, to achieve a mirror-like surface. This is harmful to old pieces, as it may remove both hallmarks and patina.

CAMPANA: A Greek vase of inverted bell shape. This style was revived in the early 19th century.

CARTOUCHE: A shape left plain to receive an engraving, normally a crest or armorial.

CASTING: The creation of an object by pouring molten silver into a mould, often made of sand. Alternatively, the lost wax method of casting uses a shape sculpted in wax and then surrounded by a stable material such as plaster. The molten metal is poured into the mould, filling the space left by the wax which melts and runs away. Both methods are used to create solid objects, as well as decorative friezes or components such as feet, spouts, and handles.

CHASING: Decoration on the surface of an object, using a blunt punch which depresses the background, leaving a raised design. No metal is removed during this process.

DIE-STAMPING: An inexpensive technique, first introduced in the late 18th century, used for mass-produced decoration. Hardened steel dies carved with designs were stamped on to sheet silver under great pressure, leaving behind a sharp image which gave the impression of hand-chasing.

EMBOSSING: Decoration by raising a design from behind using a blunt punch. No metal is removed during the process. Also called REPOUSSÉ. The end result closely resembles that achieved by chasing.

ENAMELLING: Covering the metal with a thin layer of translucent coloured glass.

ENGINE-TURNING: Machine engraving employed to create a regular pattern, often geometrical.

ENGRAVING: Decoration by cutting lines in the surface of the silver. Small particles of metal are removed by this technique.

ETCHING: Decoration produced using the corrosive effects of acid.

FASH: Small scraps and trimmings of precious metal, collected at the end of the day to be melted down and reused.

FILLED: Objects made from sheet metal filled with pitch or plaster to add both weight and strength. It is commonly used for knife handles, dressing-table pieces, and candlesticks, which may also be described as LOADED.

FINIAL: A decorative knob on the highest point of an object. This may be baluster or vase-shaped, or formed as a flower.

FLATWARE: A general term for cutlery formed from flat sheets of metal.

FLUTING: A series of ridges which may extend over part or all of an object. The flutes may be straight or spiralling.

FLY-PUNCH: A machine developed in the 18th century by the fused plate makers, to ease the task of piercing metal. It soon replaced hand-sawn piercing throughout the industry.

FRIEZE: A decorative line or border, often cast separately and then soldered into place.

FROSTING: A finely granulated decorative surface, used to form a contrast with polished silver. This type of finish may also be called SATIN or MATT.

GADROONING: A series of small flutes applied as a border decoration.

GREEK KEY: A regular, geometric design derived from classical architecture, first introduced during the neo-classical period in the 18th century and often used for borders or friezes.

HOLLOW-WARE: Hollow vessels, such as cups or bowls. The term also describes hollow knife handles.

KNOP: See FINIAL.

KNOPPED: Decorative swelling, often on a pedestal foot or candlestick.

LOADED: See FILLED.

MATT: See FROSTING.

MONOGRAM: Two or more initials which overlap, creating a complicated and decorative design.

NEO-CLASSICAL: A style of architecture which revived those of Ancient Greece, characterised by tapering, fluted columns, GREEK KEY FRIEZES, PATERAE, swags, masks, and ACANTHUS LEAVES amongst others. It was introduced in the second half of the 18th century, and subsequently enjoyed several revivals.

NICKEL SILVER: An alloy composed of about two-thirds copper, with varying amounts of nickel and zinc, much used in the manufacture of plated cutlery as well as better quality holloware.

NIELLO: Deep engraving filled with an alloy of sulphur, which was then levelled and polished to create a decorative contrasting effect.
NOZZLE: The part of a candlestick which actually holds the candle. This is usually detachable, for ease of cleaning.

PATERA: A circular or oval foliate design introduced in the neo-classical period.
PATINA: A surface gloss produced by many years of tarnish, polishing, and use, almost impossible to reproduce.
PUTTO: See AMORINO.

QUATREFOIL: A four-sided shape similar to a four-leaf clover.

REEDING: Strips of narrow grooves, usually used as border decoration.
REPOUSSÉ: See EMBOSSING.
ROCOCO: A highly ornamental style of decoration characterised by asymmetrical scrolling flowers and foliage.
RUBBING IN: A method of applying a CARTOUCHE to fused plate.

SATIN: See FROSTING.
SATYR: A horned grotesque figure, used in both rococo and later decoration.
SOLDER: A fusible alloy of metals used to join other metals with lower melting points. It is applied with a soldering iron.
SPELTER: A soft alloy composed mainly of zinc.
SPOT HAMMERING: A decorative technique which leaves behind hammer marks, usually to create a misleading impression of hand workmanship. It was much used by 19th century American metalworkers.
STERLING STANDARD: An alloy containing 925 parts of silver to 75 parts of base metal, mainly copper. This has long been the most common standard of silver in both Britain and America.
STRAPWORK: Applied or chased decoration incorporating scrolling bands of foliage.

TINNING: A process, used in the manufacture of fused plate, in which exposed copper is disguised with a thin coating of molten tin.

WRIGGLEWORK: Asymmetrical engraving or chasing, creating a textured effect.

Bibliography

GENERAL BOOKS

Army and Navy Stores Ltd., General Price list, 1935-36
Bennett, Raymond, *Collecting for Pleasure*, The Bodley Head Ltd., 1969
Bradbury, Frederick, *History of Old Sheffield Plate*, J. W. Northend Limited, 1983, reprinted from first edition of 1912
Burnett, John, editor, *Useful Toil*, Allen Lane, 1974
Bury, Shirley, *Victorian Electroplate*, Country Life Collectors' Guide
Butler, Robin and Walkling, Gillian, *The Book of Wine Antiques*, Antique Collectors' Club, 1986
Caldicott, J. W., *The Values of Old English Silver and Sheffield Plate*, Bemrose and Sons Limited, 1906
Carpenter, Charles H. Jun., *Gorham Silver, 1831-1981*, Dodd, Mead and Company, 1982
Carpenter, Charles H. Jun., and Carpenter, Mary Grace, *Tiffany Silver*, Dodd, Mead and Company, 1978
Clayton, Michael, *Christie's Pictorial History of English and American Silver*, Phaidon Christie's, 1985
Culme, John, *Nineteenth Century Silver*, Country Life Books, 1977
Frost, T.W., *The Price Guide to Old Sheffield Plate*, Antique Collectors' Club, 1971
Fennimore, Donald L., *Silver and Pewter*, Alfred A. Knopf, 1984
Hatfield, John and Julia, *The Oldest Sheffield Plater*, The Advertiser Press Limited, 1974
Hogan, Edmund P., *An American Heritage*, International Silver Company, 1977
Hogan, Edmund P., *The Elegance of Old Silverplate and some Personalities*, Schiffer Publishing Ltd., 1980
Jones, Kenneth Crisp, General Editor, *The Silversmiths of Birmingham and their Marks, 1750-1980*, NAG Press, 1981
Matthew Boulton and the Toymakers, Exhibition Catalogue, Goldsmiths Hall, 1982
May, Earl Chapin, *A Century of Silver 1847-1947*, Robert M. McBride and Company, 1947
McClinton, Katharine Morrison, *Collecting American 19th Century Silver*, Charles Scribner & Sons, 1968
Meriden Britannia Silver-Plate Treasury, Dover Publications Inc., 1982
Pickford, Ian, *Silver Flatware*, Antique Collectors' Club, 1983
Rainwater, Dorothy T. and H. Ivan, *American Silverplate*, Schiffer Publishing Ltd., 1988
Schnadig, Victor K., *American Victorian Figural Napkin Rings*, Wallace-Homestead Book Co., 1971
Schwartz, Jeri, *Silver and Silverplate*, House of Collectibles, 1989
Schwartz, Marvin D., *Collectors' Guide to American Silver*, Bonanza Books, 1975
Scott, Jack L., *Pewter Wares from Sheffield*, Antiquary Press, 1980
Silver, a bi-monthly magazine edited by Diana L. Cramer
Walker and Hall Ltd., an undated catalogue
Ward, Barbara McLean, and Ward, Gerald W.R., Editors, *Silver in American Life*, David R.Godine, 1979

BOOKS OF MARKS

Assay Office, Sheffield, *Old Silver Platers and their Marks,* second edition, 1988
Bury, Shirley, *Victorian Electroplate,* Country Life Collectors' Guides
Ensko, Stephen G.C., *American Silversmiths and their Marks,* Dover Publications Inc., published 1948, reprinted 1983
Jackson, Sir Charles, *English Goldsmiths and their Marks,* Dover reprint, 1964
Kovel, Ralph M. and Terry H., *A Directory of American Silver, Pewter, and Silverplate,* Crown Publishers Inc., 1961
Rainwater, Dorothy T., *Encyclopedia of American Silver Manufacture,* third edition revised, Schiffer Publishing Co., 1986
Wyler, Seymour B., *The Book of Old Silver,* Crown Publishers Inc., 1937
Wyler, Seymour B., *The Book of Old Sheffield Plate,* Bonanza Books, 1949

ELKINGTON & Cº